EQ5 COLOR

Applying Color Theory to Quilts By Susan McKelvey

The Electric Quilt Company
419 Gould Street, Suite 2
Bowling Green, OH 43402

The Electric Quilt Company
419 Gould Street, Suite 2
Bowling Green, OH 43402-3047
419-352-1134
E-mail: sales@electricquilt.com
Web site: www.electricquilt.com

Credits

Editor:	Andrea Poulimenos
Cover Design:	Jill Badenhop
Book Design:	Sara Layne, Rachel Reulbach
Technical Reviewers:	Penny McMorris, Angie Maidment, Heidi Thieman, Sara Pfeifer, Margaret Okuley, Monica Vay
Technical Help:	Ann Rutter

Quilt design shown on front cover designed by Susan McKelvey.

EQ5 Color

Acknowledgements

When the folks at EQ and I began this book, I knew that I knew color and quilt design, but not the ins and outs of the wonderful possibilities when using the EQ design program for color theory.

Thanks to the vision of Penny and Dean and the patience of my editor, Andrea, and her assistants, Sara and Rachel, the lessons are wonderful and the writing and editing process was fun.

Introduction

EQ5 Color: An Easy Way to Learn Color Theory

"We hear, and we forget,

We see, and we remember,

We do, and it is ours forever."

To learn how colors interact, we must play with colors. I began to study color theory in 1982 when I started designing quilts. A non-artist, I wanted to know the how and why of design and color. The things I found out were marvelous and got me started on a long and colorful journey.

For all of these years as I taught color, we pasted snippets of fabric and colored with markers, worthy but slow methods for illustrating color effects. And of course, we made quilts, even worthier and slower!

Then along came The Electric Quilt Company. When I began playing with quilt design in Electric Quilt, I immediately realized its potential for studying color theory. The very characteristics that make quilt design on EQ so easy can make color study easy, too. Now we can paste and change colors at the touch of the mouse! We can see the principles of color theory in the wink of an eyedropper. True colors, real fabrics, limitless quilt layouts — all are at our fingertips. We can save the quilts we make in our own personal Sketchbooks, creating a slide show of color theory examples, which can be an invaluable learning tool.

Pre-EQ, the old cut and paste fabric method was our only option. With EQ, coloring is fast, and we can amass and save a wealth of quilts as examples of each color principle.

It has been great fun to design the many projects for your color experimentation. All of the directions are step-by-step and easy to follow. I hope you will use them to study color and enjoy the experience.

Susan McKelvey

On Maryland's Chesapeake Bay

2003

Table of Contents

Color Comes First

Chapter 1

Color Comes First!

1

Color in quilts, as in all art, is what strikes the viewer first. It is the impact of a quilt's color that attracts or repels us, that leads us to examine other elements of the quilt. The stitching may be exquisite and the piecing flawless, but unless the colors are compelling, the quilt fails to command our attention.

Color, then, is the grabber, the eyecatcher, the lure. It is not the specific color that matters — a red quilt will grab you even if red is not your favorite color. It is the power of the color that catches the eye. Once caught, you may savor any number of a quilt's qualities — workmanship, number of stitches per inch, complexity of piecing, mitered corners, or design originality. But these are close-up judgements. Color comes first!

Since color use can make or break a quilt, it is not enough to trust your intuition or use your favorite colors — at least not once you are beyond your first quilt. Serious quilters enjoy treating color seriously.

Color theory applies to quilts. The quilts we love are memorable precisely because, consciously or unconsciously, their makers used valid and established color principles. You, too, can use these principles. They are logical and understandable. There are terms you must learn, but here we present them in logical order, with simple explanations and easy projects. By the time you have read and worked through the projects in EQ5 Color, you will be prepared to meet the color challenge.

How to Study Color in EQ

About the Lessons

• For every color concept, I have included one or more lessons.

• You need to *work through the lessons in order* because we add terms and concepts as you go. Don't rush or skip around at this stage. In a sense, the first few lessons may be the most difficult, because all the information may be new and the process of designing may be new, too. But, after you finish the introductory lessons, the rest of the book should be a piece of cake.

• In each lesson, I guide you through the design process step-by-step. I direct you to study the quilts at certain points so you see the results of what you have done. Each lesson ends with a summary section called *Study the Quilts and Remember What You Learned*. Use this to review and remember the lesson's color concept and how it applies to quilt design.

• In some lessons, I recommend other quilts for further practice, quilts which exemplify the color concept. These quilts are optional, but use this as a chance to practice the technique you learned, without my telling you where to put the color.

• In the Reference section, I give you a list of blocks that lend themselves well to different color concepts — just in case you are as eager as I am to continue experimenting once you have finished the book.

• You may be wondering why a color book would ever be produced in black and white. Going through these lessons is a chance for *you* to experiment with color and see their interactions. I don't want the way *I* color blocks to affect *your* coloring decisions. Keeping this book in black and white trains your eye and is the easiest way to keep your designs within the guidelines of the lessons, without my telling you exactly which color to put where.

Color is a Long-Distance Illusion So Sit Back to See Color

In my lectures and classes, I tell students to stand back at least 5 feet to see color rather than line. I even recommend squinting or taking off their glasses to eliminate line (with luck, only color comes through the blur!). Sitting at the computer, however, you can't sit back 5 feet. Since the quilts you are making on the computer are small, leaning back as far as you can is fine. Lean back, even get up and stretch, take off your glasses, and look at color only.

The Quilts You Design Show Multiple Color Concepts

By the time you finish the lessons in this book, you will have a treasury of quilts you can review at any time. Although each set of quilts was designed to illustrate a specific color concept, the individual quilts also show other concepts. At your leisure, try strolling down memory lane through your Sketchbooks and analyze the quilts for *all the color interactions happening simultaneously*.

About the Sketchbook

1

The Sketchbook has four tabs: Quilts, Blocks, Fabrics, and Colors. Click a tab to see what's there. The Sketchbook is your project. Use the arrows and/or scrollbars to go through the items on that tab. If you do not see something in your Sketchbook, it is not part of your project yet. You need to copy the item from the library or save the design in your Sketchbook to make it part of your project.

Save Each Quilt You Design in the Sketchbook

In each lesson, you will be changing the quilts frequently. EQ provides you with the opportunity to save as many quilts as you want in the Sketchbook. Be sure to *save all versions of a quilt*. These will form a wealth of examples of the concept you have worked on.

Rule: **Change a color — Click Save in Sketchbook.**

You can always go through the Sketchbook later and eliminate the quilts you don't want to keep. But ponder this: *You learn just as much from unsuccessful examples as from successful, so be cautious about deleting quilts.*

The Sketchbook Provides the Best Quilt Show in Town

The EQ Sketchbook is the true gift to learning about color! As you play, you are creating unparalleled and original examples of color concepts. Not only do you practice, you can save all the quilts you make. In no other learning format can you do this. What a gift: a collection of examples of a concept at your fingertips, a set of quilts you can add to as you learn and continue to experiment. View your Sketchbook, click the Quilts tab, and click the arrows to scroll through your quilts. Use your personal quilt show to the max — for review, for study, for enjoyment and perhaps as the inspiration for a real quilt.

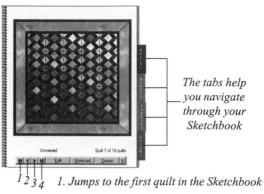

The tabs help you navigate through your Sketchbook

1. Jumps to the first quilt in the Sketchbook
2. Scrolls back to the previous quilt
3. Scrolls forward to the next quilt
4. Jumps to the last quilt in the Sketchbook

Use the Save in Sketchbook button often

The Sketchbook is the best place to display the many changes you can make to a quilt using colors

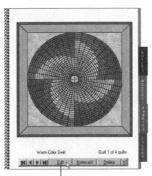

Click Edit to send the quilt you see to the worktable so you may make your changes

Not only is it beneficial to label your quilts on the Notecard, but it is also good to write as much information as you can: what blocks or fabric styles you used, what color concepts are shown, whether the quilt is successful or not, etc.

Click the Save button to make your Notecard changes permanent

How to Change to a Different Quilt from the Sketchbook (EDIT)

Sometimes the quilts change greatly as you work through a lesson, and the last quilt in the Sketchbook looks nothing like the first. When you open the Sketchbook, the last quilt saved always appears. But what if you want to play with the design of an earlier quilt? All you need to do is edit the quilt. Use the arrows to scroll through the Sketchbook until you find the quilt design you want to modify, click the Edit button, and that quilt will appear on the worktable, ready for change.

This method applies when you open an existing project, too. Find the quilt you would like to play with in the Sketchbook, click Edit, and the quilt is ready for you.

Then, if you make changes to the quilt, don't forget to click the Save in Sketchbook button.

How and Why to Use the Notecards

When you finish a lesson, take time to label the quilts you made. As you flip through the quilts under the Sketchbook's Quilts tab, click the Notecard button, write a title that means something to you, and close it. Click the Save button once you close the Notecard and the Sketchbook to make your changes permanent. *You won't regret labelling your quilts when you return weeks later to a lesson to review a color concept.*

Worktable Methods

How to Get a Block Quickly By Name

What do you do when you remember seeing a great block, but you don't remember where it was? What if I ask you to use a specific block in a lesson, but you don't want to click through all the pages to find it? In either case, you search for the block. *EQ has a great Search feature in the Block Library that lets you search by block name.* Just click Libraries — Block Library to open the library, then click Search. Type in what you are looking for and click the Search button on this box.

Block and Border Sizes

Block size usually doesn't matter for these lessons, especially when you work with solids. Sometimes I have designed quilts with large blocks when it is important to see more of a print fabric. The quilts are set up to be a pleasing proportion on your screen, not necessarily the size at which you would actually make the quilt. When you design your own quilts, keep this in mind: If you decide to actually make one of the quilts, you will, of course, want to change the sizes of the blocks and possibly the borders.

How to Enlarge the Fabrics Palette

The Fabrics palette sits at the right of the screen. It's often helpful to enlarge it so you can see the detail in fabrics, especially prints. Do this after you have finished setting up the quilt on the Layout and Borders tabs. Once you are on Layer 1, you can see whether any open space is left on the screen. To enlarge the palette, place the cursor over the upper-left corner of the palette. A double-ended diagonal arrow will appear. Click and drag this corner up and to the left for placement. Drag the bottom-right corner down and to the right to increase the size even more. Now you can see more of the pattern and texture detail in the fabrics.

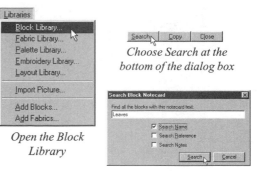

Open the Block Library

Choose Search at the bottom of the dialog box

Type the name that you want to search

This header displays how many blocks have been found in the search

You can change the number of blocks displayed by clicking on one of these buttons

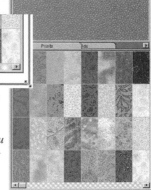

Stretching the palette by pulling both corners to make the palette as large as you can helps you see the fabrics more easily

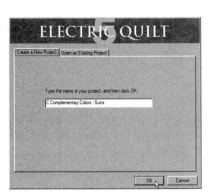

Name your quilt with a descriptive name, then click OK

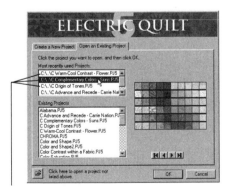

Keep your projects organized by making all your projects of the same lesson begin with the same title, then add a more specific subtitle to distinguish it from the rest

Terms I Use

• *Choose:* find and click on.

• *Columns:* go up and down.

• *Rows:* go across.

• *CTRL + click:* Hold down the Control (CTRL) key on your keyboard as you click with the mouse. CTRL + click does a replacement in every matching patch. If you are setting blocks, it sets the block in every space. If you are coloring a patch in a block, it colors every matching patch.

• *ALT + click:* Hold down the Alternate (ALT) key on your keyboard as you click with the mouse. ALT + click does the replacement in every other one. If you are setting blocks, it sets the block in every other block space. If you are coloring a patch in a block, it colors every other patch in matching blocks.

Name Each Lesson When You Save It

EQ lists the projects in alphabetical order and allows a long title. You will name each lesson when you save it. Rather than naming it Lesson 1, try to make it as descriptive as possible. In this book, we've tried to put the letter C, the concept name, and then a description of the block or quilt into the title. This way all your color projects will be together under "C", and you'll know the concept or quilt design before you even reopen a project.

For example, would you rather see this first name or second name, when you're searching through your projects?:

• *C Complementary Colors - Suns*
• *Lesson 5: Complementary Colors*

You may do several quilts that illustrate complementary contrast, each with different quilts. This will make finding the concept easy and keep all the projects on each concept together in the list.

Using Fabrics in the Library

How to Choose Fabrics

EQ provides you with hundreds of real quilt fabrics to play with. This makes the quilts you design look real, and truly exemplifies how beautiful quilts depend upon a variety of prints for their punch.

In each lesson, I guide you through the process of choosing fabrics appropriate for that concept. ***Take the time to choose the fabrics and <u>always</u> <u>choose more than you will need.</u>*** If you like the group of fabrics you have collected, save it as a palette of your own at the end.

Creating Your Own Palette

Fabrics in EQ can be found in one of two places. You can get fabrics one-by-one from the Fabric Library or in a group from the Palette Library.

To copy a fabric from the Fabric Library, click the fabric to select it and click the Copy button. Click Close when you are finished collecting fabrics.

To load a palette from the Palette Library, click the name of the palette to select it, then click the Load button. You can also load palettes you've already created and saved. Just click the My Palettes tab that is behind the EQ5 Palettes tab. Once you click Load, you will have the opportunity to choose what you want to do with the current fabrics in your Sketchbook — if you don't know which one to choose, just click OK.

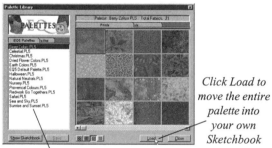

2. Make a fabric selection

1. Choose a category

3. Click Copy to move the selected fabric to your palette

Click Load to move the entire palette into your own Sketchbook

Choose a palette from the EQ5 Palettes

Choosing a palette that you have already created and saved is a good way to get a large collection of your favorite fabrics at one time instead of one-by-one

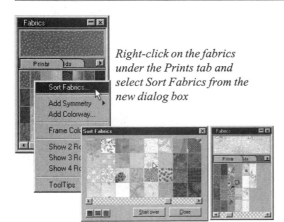

Right-click on the fabrics under the Prints tab and select Sort Fabrics from the new dialog box

Choose the order of your fabrics by clicking one-by-one on the fabrics in the Sort box

1. Click the My Palettes tab

3. Click Save

2. Choose Show Sketchbook

Give your new palette a descriptive name and click Save

EQ5 Pa | My Palettes
Pure Colors and Values.PL5
Sara's Warm Fabrics.PL5
Tones of Pure Colors.PL5

Your newly created palette will now show up on the My Palettes tab of the Palette Library

Sort Your Fabrics

When you collect fabrics from the libraries you may notice all your red prints are everywhere in the palette and your blue prints are all over the place as well. To organize your fabrics, you can sort them. With the Fabrics palette in front of you, right-click on top of the prints and choose Sort Fabrics. In the new box that appears, click the fabrics in the order you want them. Click Start Over if you make a mistake. Click Close when you are finished or if you want EQ5 to put the remaining fabrics in their current order at the end of the already sorted prints.

Save Your Own Palette

So you have an amazing collection of fabrics in your current project, but you want to have it available in other projects. What do you do? Save the current group of fabrics as a palette in your very own Palette Library. Click Libraries — Palette Library and then the My Palettes tab (behind the EQ5 Palettes tab). Click Show Sketchbook, so you see all the fabrics in your current project. Click Save. Type a descriptive name to remind you of what is in the set. Don't name it Palette 1; instead say Large Florals or Many Greens. Click the Save button. You can then use these palettes for any future project.

1

Design Principles for All Quilts

1

Line and shape are a major part of design. When we design quilts, we can follow basic art design principles. You will work through the color concepts in each chapter, but as you play with color, keep these principles in mind.

Create Movement

Movement can be:

- From left to right, which follows the direction we read in Western culture

- On a diagonal from top-left to bottom-right or from bottom-left to top-right

- Horizontal or vertical

- Gradual change or gradation in size, color or shape

In this quilt, there are three lighter colors running on diagonals to show movement in the design

Include Repetition & Variety

Repetition of color, line, shape and size helps create movement and ties the elements of a quilt together. A color or a shape can lead the viewer's eye across the quilt.

Variety adds interest. We are used to variety in fabric prints, but often the block structure of traditional quilt design limits variety in patch sizes. Focus instead on adding variety in line.

Integrate the Quilt Borders

Consider the borders your quilt's finishing touch. They are not an afterthought but an integral part of the quilt. Their size should be in proportion to that of the center. Repeat colors and designs from the center.

You will work with multiple borders in many of the lessons. By the end of your study, you will have experimented a great deal with the process of integrating borders into quilts.

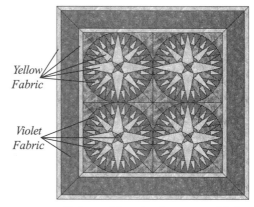

Yellow Fabric

Violet Fabric

All three of these borders repeat fabrics from the quilt center which helps to connect the quilt together as a whole

CHAPTER 1
The Color Wheel

It is necessary to begin to build a vocabulary with which to discuss color. Let's start with the basic structure of color — the color wheel. Our color wheel is a twelve-color wheel. It is the most familiar wheel, and gives us the information we need.

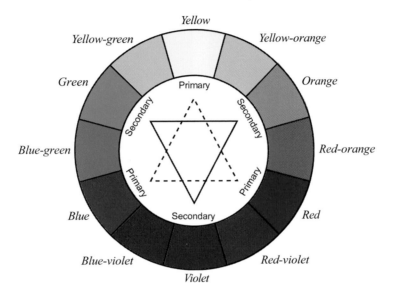

Primary Colors
Many of you will remember from elementary school that there are three *primary colors*: red, yellow and blue. These are called *primary* because it is from these three that all other colors are mixed. Notice on the color wheel that these are positioned at the three points of an equilateral triangle.

Secondary Colors
There are three *secondary colors*: orange, green and violet (purple). They are the second set of colors and are simple combinations of the *primary colors*:

Red + yellow = orange

Yellow + blue = green

Blue + red = violet (purple)

Tertiary Colors
The colors made by combining primary and secondary colors are called *tertiary colors*, or the third set of colors. Mix blue and green to get blue-green, green and yellow to get yellow-green, continuing around the wheel. The term *tertiary* isn't as important as is the knowledge that all the colors on the color wheel are mixed from the first *primary* colors.

CHAPTER 2
The Color Wheel and Introduction to Value and Saturation

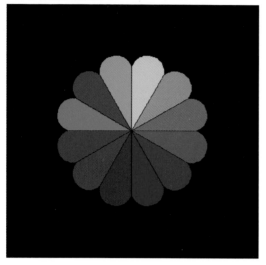

Color wheel with twelve colors on a black background

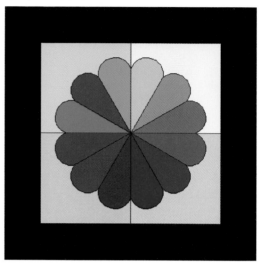

Echo colors in the background to give a transparent look

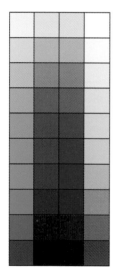

Value scale for four colors

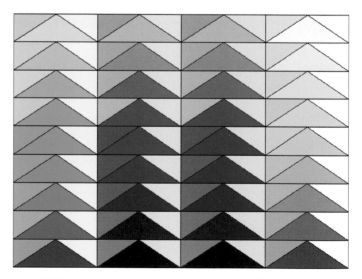

Value versus saturation comparison in flying geese

PAGES 22 & 32

CHAPTER 2
The Origin of Tones

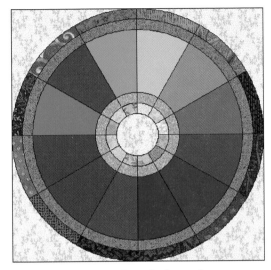

Use gray bands to find toned prints

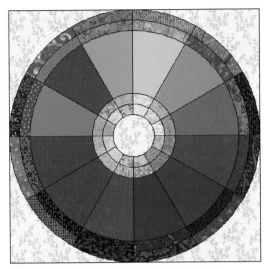

Solid color wheel with four tones per color

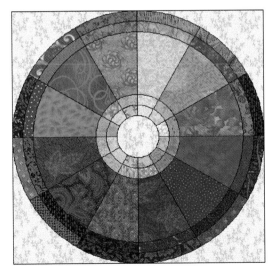

Pure prints and four of their tones on a light background

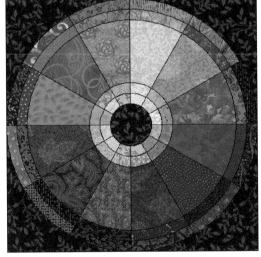

Pure prints and four of their tones on a dark background

PAGE 42

19

CHAPTER 2
How Much Chroma?

An achromatic quilt is without color (black, white, and gray only)

A monochromatic quilt has one color and its values

A polychromatic quilt contains more than one color

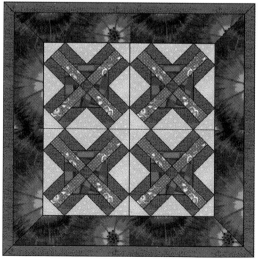

A polychromatic quilt in blue-green, rust and their values

PAGE 48

The Color Wheel

Chapter 2

Setting Up The Color Wheel

Color Theory

The color wheel was designed to provide a visual reference for discussing color theory. The standard artist's color wheel contains twelve colors in a circle. Each color has a name. We can point to a color on the color wheel, call it by name, and know that we are talking about the same thing.

2

We have provided an accurate color wheel on page 17 to which you can refer often. But it is fun and easy to design one of your own, too. Working through this lesson will impress the color wheel upon your mind.

Let's Create Your Own Color Wheel

1   Start EQ5.

2   Choose Create a New Project.

3   Type the name for your new project: C Color Wheel.

4   Click OK.

5   On the top menu bar, click Worktable — Work on Quilt.

Design the Quilt

Layout

6   Click Quilt — New Quilt — Horizontal.

7   Click the Layout tab along the bottom of the screen.

8   Under Number of blocks, click the arrows to read 1 Horizontal and 1 Vertical.

9   Under Size of blocks, drag the sliders to read 10.00 Width and 10.00 Height. Don't worry about Sashing because there is only one block.

Borders

10   Click the Borders tab along the bottom of the screen.

Step 1

Step 2-4

Step 5

Step 6

Step 7

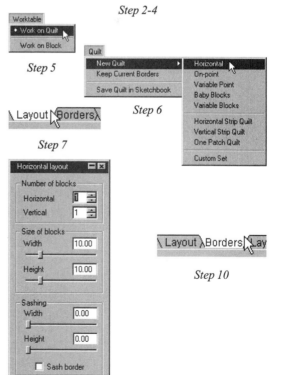

Step 8-9

Step 10

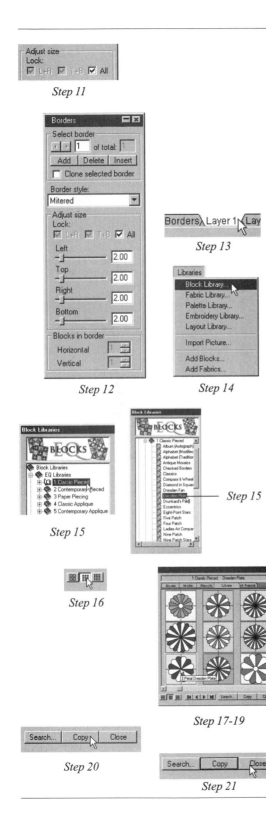

Step 11

Step 12

Step 13

Step 14

Step 15

Step 15

Step 16

Step 17-19

Step 20

Step 21

2

11 Be sure there is a check next to All under Adjust Size. (Clicking will turn this check on and off.)

12 Drag one of the sliders to 2.00. All sides of the border will adjust automatically.

13 Click the Layer 1 tab along the bottom of the screen.

Block

14 Click Libraries — Block Library on the top menu bar.

15 Inside the library, click EQ Libraries — 1 Classic Pieced — Dresden Plate. The blocks in this book will appear on the right.

16 Click the View 9 blocks at a time button at the bottom of the Block Library.

17 Drag the horizontal scrollbar below the block to the right to see all the blocks in this book.

18 You want the 3 Petal Dresden Plate block, which is the bottom block in the first column. Position the mouse cursor over a block (without clicking) and the block name will appear. This tooltip helps you find a block by its name.

19 Click on the 3 Petal Dresden Plate block to select it. You'll see a frame around it to know it's the selected one.

20 Click Copy. You'll notice that the block temporarily disappears, indicating you've "copied" it into your Sketchbook.

21 Click Close. Now you're back to the Quilt Worktable and ready to set blocks.

22 Click the Set tool, then the Blocks tab. The Block page of the Sketchbook appears, showing the 3 Petal Dresden Place block. Click on the block to select it.

23 Position your cursor over the block space in your empty quilt layout and click. Your quilt is now filled with the block.

Color the Color Wheel

Go to page 17 and study the color wheel. The colors are what we call *pure colors*. This means they are intense and saturated with color. They are the strongest versions of themselves.

The standard artist's color wheel has twelve pie wedges. We are using the 3 Petal Dresden Plate because it, too, has twelve pie wedges. You will now make your own Dresden Plate Color Wheel, using twelve pure colors from the Basic EQ Palette.

Primary Colors

24 Click the Paintbrush tool. The EQ fabric palette will appear.

25 Click the Solids tab on the palette. Scroll to the right and left to see all the colors available.

26 Leave your cursor over a color for a second (without clicking), and the color's identification number will appear.

27 Find and click on **white** (R:255 G:255 B:255). Click in all the wedges of your 3 Petal Dresden Plate so that it is colored white.

28 Now begin to put colors onto your quilt with yellow at the top-right of the wheel. Refer to the color wheel on page 17 whenever you need to. Find and click on the pure, bright **yellow** (R:255 G:204 B:0). Place the cursor over the top-right wedge and click. The wedge will fill with yellow.

29 Find and click on the pure **red** (R:255 G:0 B:0) in the palette.

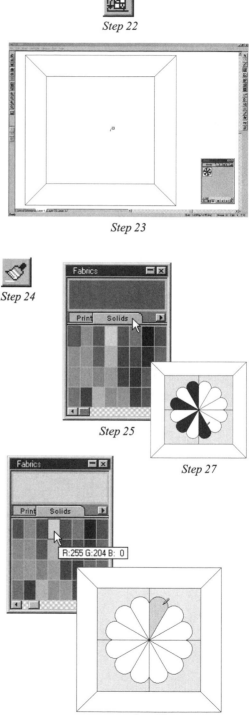

Step 22

Step 23

Step 24

Step 25

Step 27

Step 28

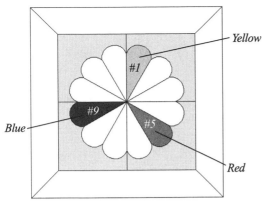

Steps 30-31

30 Look at your color wheel so far. Let's call yellow Wedge #1. Count clockwise around the wheel and click in Wedge #5. It will now be colored red.

31 Find and click on the pure **blue** in the palette (R:0 G:0 B:255). Counting the red Wedge as #5, count clockwise around the wheel again and click in Wedge #9. It will fill with blue.

32 Click the Save in Sketchbook button to save this quilt to your project.

Step 32

Look at the block with only three wedges colored. Notice how the three colors are evenly spaced five spaces from each other. These are the three *primary colors*, which are equidistant from each other and form the points of an equilateral triangle. Many of you will remember these three primary colors from your elementary school art classes: red, yellow and blue. They are called primary because it is from these three that all twelve colors on the color wheel and, in fact, all other colors are mixed.

Secondary Colors

Let's mix the primary colors to form the second set of colors: orange, green and violet. These are called the *secondary colors* and are evenly spaced between the primary colors on the color wheel.

Red + yellow = orange

Yellow + blue = green

Blue + red = violet

33 Find and click on the pure **orange** in the palette (R:247 G:107 B:3). Click to set it halfway between yellow and red on your Dresden Plate. (If yellow is Wedge #1, orange is Wedge #3.)

34 Find and click on pure **violet** (R:123 G:3 B:171) and set it halfway between red and blue (in Wedge #7).

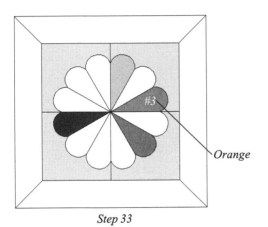

Step 33

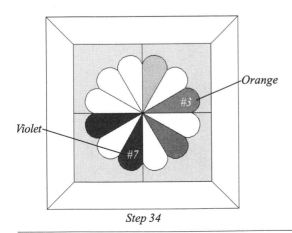

Step 34

2

35 Next, find and click on pure **green** (R:0 G:98 B:0) and set it halfway between blue and yellow in Wedge #11.

36 Click the Save in Sketchbook button to save this quilt to your project.

Tertiary Colors

The colors made by combining the primary and secondary colors are called *tertiary colors,* or the third set of colors. There are six of them. Mix blue and green to get blue-green, green and yellow to get yellow-green, continuing around the wheel. The term tertiary isn't as important as is the knowledge that all the colors on the color wheel are mixed from the first three primary colors.

37 Work clockwise around the circle, filling the wedges left with the tertiary colors. See if you can find the right color yourself, then check it against the color wheel pictured on page 17 and the number listed below. Sometimes there are several good possibilities. Just remember: pure = bright, intense and saturated with color.

> **Yellow-orange** (R:255 G:153 B:O)
>
> **Red-orange** (R:253 G:79 B:4)
>
> **Red-violet** (R:204 G:0 B:102)
>
> **Blue-violet** (R:102 G:51 B:204)
>
> **Blue-green** (R:0 G:153 B:153)
>
> **Yellow-green** (R:109 G:181 B:2)

38 Find and click on **white** in the palette. Make the background pure white by clicking in each corner.

39 Let's make the border **black**. Click on the black swatch in the palette, hold down the control key (CTRL) on your keyboard, and click on one border section. All four sides will fill at the same time because you used the CTRL key. You have now created an accurate color wheel.

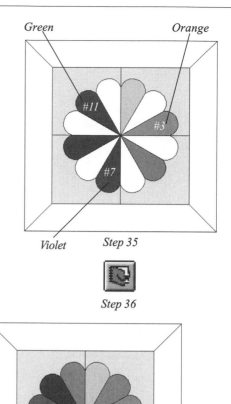

Green   *Orange*

Violet   *Step 35*

Step 36

Step 37

Steps 38-39

Step 40

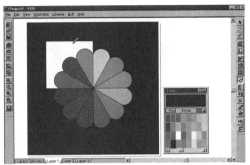

Steps 41-42

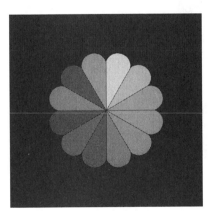

Step 43

Step 44

40 Click the Save in Sketchbook to save your color wheel in this project.

Warm and Cool Colors

Of the twelve colors on the color wheel, six are warm and six are cool. The warm colors — the yellow, oranges and reds of fire and the sun — are on the right side of the wheel. The cool colors — the blues and greens of the sea and sky — are on the left side. We will cover the concept of color temperature in later lessons, but it is important to know that the colors on the color wheel are always organized in this way: warm on one side and cool on the other. The sides may be reversed, but the warm colors remain juxtaposed with the cool.

Let's Play with the Color Wheel

You are now going to play with the background of your color wheel. After each change is complete, save it in the Sketchbook. This will give you a variety of examples. After each change, lean back to get a bit of distance from the computer and see how this simple change of background and border alters how the colors on the wheel color look.

41 Click on the **black** swatch in the Solids palette.

42 Click on each of the four background corners of the block. This change will make the color wheel float on a large black background.

43 Sit back and notice how the black background makes the pure colors seem brighter. Black always intensifies pure colors and "makes them sing."

44 Save this version of the color wheel in the Sketchbook.

2

45 Pick a **light color** in the palette. Color all four corners of the block. Leave the black border. Try several, including a **light blue** and a **light pink**.

46 Save each in your Sketchbook.

✎ Tip

If you accidentally click a patch you don't want to recolor, choose EDIT-Undo from the top menu bar immediately. You can also use the keyboard shortcut CTRL + Z to undo a mistake.

2

47 Put different colors in each of the four background sections. In each section, use the pastel versions of one of the three colors in that section. Try These:

Pale yellow in the top-right section (R:255 G:255 B:153)

Pale red (pink) in the bottom-right section (R:255 G:204 B:255)

Pale blue in the bottom-left section (R:204 G:204 B:255)

Pale green in the top-left section (R:204 G:255 B:153)

Notice how using these light versions of the pure colors gives the color wheel quilt an almost transparent look.

48 Click the Save in Sketchbook button.

Step 45

Step 46

Pale Green   *Pale Yellow*

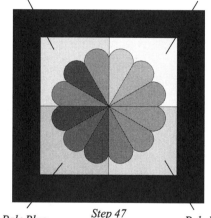

Pale Blue   *Step 47*   *Pale Red*

Step 48

Step 49

Step 50

Step 51

Click to skip to the first quilt in the Sketchbook   Click to move one-by-one through the Sketchbook

Play with the Border of the Color Wheel

You are now going to play with the border of your color wheel. Keep the four-color background of the last color wheel you saved.

49 Try different **pure colors** in the border from the center wheel. Hold down the CTRL key on your keyboard while you click in the border, to color all four sides at the same time. Each border change will alter which colors on the wheel stand out because you have changed the proportion of one color, which makes it stronger.

50 Save each version in the Sketchbook.

51 When you are finished, click the Save button to save your project.

Study Your Quilts

• Click the View Sketchbook button to open your Sketchbook. Click the Quilts tab. It is most useful to view the quilts in the order you made them so they form a progression of examples. To do this, click the first arrow on the left. This takes you to the first quilt in this project. Use the third arrow to go one by one through the quilts in this project. This overview of the finished quilts gives you a wealth of identical designs changed only by color.

• As you flip through the Sketchbook, notice how different the pure colors of the wheel look on a white background and a black background.

• Notice how different colors stand out when you change the background and border. If you added a light blue border, you brought out the blue. If you added a pink, you emphasized the reds. By increasing the quantity of the color, you made it stronger.

2

Remember What You Learned

- The standard color wheel contains twelve colors.

- The colors on the color wheel are pure colors, intense and saturated.

- The six warm colors are the colors of fire and the sun. The six cool colors are the colors of the grass, the sky and the sea.

- The warm and cool colors are on opposite sides of the color wheel.

2

- The primary, secondary and tertiary colors make up these 12 colors of the color wheel.

- Primary colors are the three basic pure colors from which all other colors on the wheel are mixed.

- The secondary colors are mixed from the primary colors.

- You make tertiary colors by combining the primary and secondary colors.

- The color of the background and border can alter how a quilt looks.

- Black makes pure colors sing!

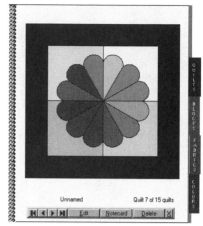

Final Sketchbook Quilts

2

Understanding Pure Colors, Values and Tones

Color Theory

This lesson introduces several other useful concepts and terms you need to know about the colors on the color wheel.

Hues & Colors

The color wheel contains twelve distinct colors (also called hues). These are the primary, secondary, and tertiary colors we learned about in the first lesson. I use the word color, not hue, throughout this book.

Pure Colors

The colors on our wheel are all clear, strong and saturated; the reddest red and the bluest blue possible. They are what we call pure colors. We can change these pure colors in two ways: in value and in saturation.

Values

If we take any one of the pure colors and make it darker or lighter, we are playing with value. If we were mixing paints, we would add black or white.

- **Darker** versions of a color are called shades.

- **Lighter** versions of a color are called tints.

- There can be **many** gradations of value levels in any color.

Shade is a term we already know and use frequently. If a friend says she used several shades of blue in her quilt, we know immediately what she means. She may have used navy, royal blue and baby blue but calls them shades of blue. If she were using color terms more precisely, she would say there were three values of blue — a shade (navy), pure blue (royal blue) and a tint (baby blue). But whichever she says, quilters understand that it was a blue quilt, containing three values.

Value, then, is a concept with which we are all familiar.

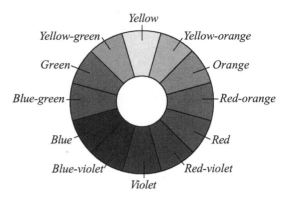

Pure Colors of the Color Wheel

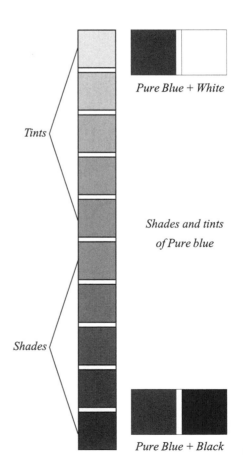

Pure Blue + White

Shades and tints of Pure blue

Pure Blue + Black

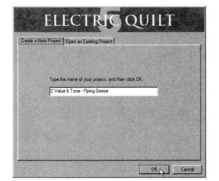

Steps 2-4

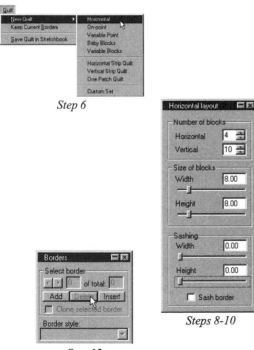

Step 6

Steps 8-10

Step 12

Saturation

The colors on the color wheel are pure colors. To say it another way, they are strong, intense, and saturated with color. If we take any one of these pure colors and add gray to it, the color becomes weaker, less vibrant, or muted. Whenever we add gray to a color, we are changing the color's saturation. It then becomes a tone or "grayed version" of its pure color. Think of the phrase "to tone down"; that's what we do when we change saturation.

Let's Make a Value Scale

1   Start EQ5.

2   Choose Create a New Project.

3   Type the name for your new project: C Value & Tone - Flying Geese.

4   Click OK.

5   Click Worktable — Work on Quilt.

Design the Value Scale
Layout

6   Click Quilt — New Quilt — Horizontal.

7   Click the Layout tab along the bottom of the screen.

8   Under Number of blocks, click the arrows to read 4 Horizontal and 10 Vertical.

9   Under Size of blocks, drag the sliders to read 8.00 Width and 8.00 Height.

10 Under Sashing, drag both sliders to read 0.00 to eliminate the sashing.

Borders

11 Click the Borders tab along the bottom of the screen.

12 Click the Delete button to eliminate all borders.

13 Click the Layer 1 tab.

2

Collect the Fabrics for the Value Scale

14 Click the Paintbrush tool. The Fabrics palette appears.

15 Click the Solids tab.

16 Click on the scrollbar at the bottom of the palette and drag it to the left and right to see all of the colors.

17 Click on **any color you like**, so it is selected.

18 Right-click on it and click Add Shades and Tints.

19 The Add Shades and Tints box will appear. You will see ten values of that color. Click the Add to Sketchbook button.

20 Scroll through the Solids Palette to see that the ten new values have been placed at the far right end. Notice that they are in order of value from dark on the left to light on the right.

21 Repeat Steps 17-20 for **three other colors you like**, striving for variety. Now your four sets have been added to the far-right end of the solids.

Color the Value Scale

You are ready to put the colors into your quilt. Look at your quilt. There are four columns of ten squares each. You are going to put ten values of one color in each column. It will be easiest to color from top to bottom.

22 Choose one of your color sets. Remember: placing the values in order in a column is easy because they are already arranged in order of value.

Step 14

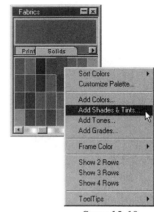

Steps 15-18

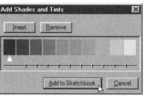

Step 19

Step 21

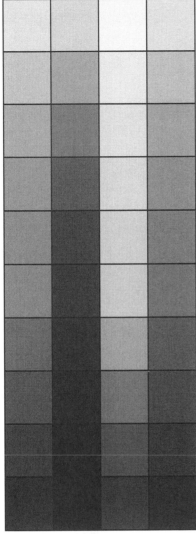

Steps 23-25

Step 26

23 Click on the **lightest tint** of that color and place it in the top square of any column.

24 Click and place each value of the color into the column, going in order from tints at the top to shades at the bottom.

25 Follow the same procedure for the three remaining color sets.

26 Click the Save in Sketchbook button to save this Value Scale.

Tip _____

The scrollbar at the bottom of the Fabrics palette can be used to scroll through the swatches. If you click once on the left arrow (not the bar in between), it will take you one by one backward through the swatches. If you click the lightest tint of a color, color the quilt then click the left arrow, you will now be on the second-lightest color.

Study the Value Scale & Remember What You Learned

• Value refers to the lightness or darkness of a color.

• You have now made a sample containing four value scales, each of which runs from dark at the bottom to light at the top.

• EQ makes finding value gradations of any solid color easy: just click on the color, choose Add Tints and Shades from the pop up menu, and voila!

Let's Make a Quilt out of the Value Scales: Flying Geese Gradations

Since you have your value scales added to the solids, let's use them to make a simple Flying Geese quilt.

Start a New Quilt

Layout

27 Click Quilt — New Quilt — Horizontal on the top menu bar. Your colored quilt will disappear because we are starting a new quilt, but remember it has been saved in the Sketchbook and is available for your review at any time.

28 Click the Layout tab along the bottom of your screen.

29 Under Number of blocks, click the arrows to read 4 Horizontal and 3 Vertical.

30 Under Size of blocks, drag the sliders to read 8.00 Width and 8.00 Height.

31 Under Sashing, drag both sliders to read 0.00 to eliminate sashing.

Borders

32 Click the Borders tab along the bottom of the screen.

33 Click the Delete button. This way we only have the quilt center and no borders.

34 Click the Layer 1 tab along the bottom of your screen.

Block

35 Click Libraries — Block Library — EQ Libraries — 3 Paper Piecing — Flying Geese. The blocks will appear on the right.

36 Scroll through the blocks. To find a block's name, place your cursor over a block without clicking on it.

37 Find and click on the Flying Geese IV block. (If your view is still set to 9 blocks at a time, it is the center block.)

38 Click Copy.

39 Click Close. You're back on the quilt worktable.

40 Click the Set tool, then the Blocks tab.

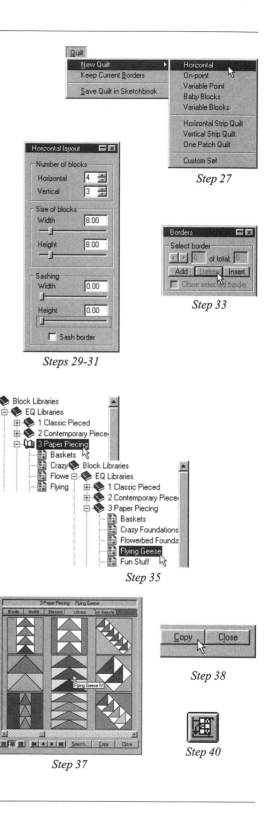

Step 27

Steps 29-31

Step 33

Step 35

Step 37

Step 38

Step 40

Step 43

Second-lightest value

Third-lightest value

Fourth-lightest value

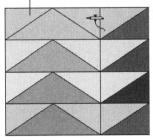

Steps 45-46

Lightest value

Step 47

Step 49

41 Click the Flying Geese IV block to select it.

42 Hold down the CTRL key on your keyboard and click in any block in the quilt. You now have a Flying Geese quilt with four columns.

43 Click the Spraycan tool (not the EQ4 Spraycan tool). The Fabrics palette appears. Your four value sets are still at the very end.

✎ Tip _____

The Paintbrush tool colors one patch at a time. The Spraycan tool sprays all like-colored patches in a block. This means less coloring time if you want them all the same color.

You will use the four colors and their values in the quilt. Each column will hold the value scale of one color. Notice that you have ten values but only nine geese (the center triangles). Follow the directions below for placement.

44 Begin working with any color in any column.

45 Begin by placing the **second-lightest value** in the top goose triangle.

46 Work downward, filling the geese triangles with successively darker values, placing the darkest at the bottom. Use the tip after Step 26 to make your coloring time go faster.

47 Put the **very lightest value** of the color you are working with in all the background spaces (outer triangles of the blocks) of the column by clicking piece by piece down the column.

48 Repeat Steps 45 - 47 for each color, but in the other columns.

49 Click the Save in Sketchbook button.

50 You now have a quilt designed around gradation of value.

2

Gradation of Value Quilt

Study *Flying Geese Gradations* and Remember What you have Learned

- You turned a gradation of values into a simple quilt.

- In this quilt, there is only value to create visual interest and movement. But value is enough!

- Which colors stand out the most in the quilt? If you said the purest colors in the quilt's center stand out, you are correct.

- A Tried & True Design Formula: I directed you to put the darks at the bottom and lights at the top because it is a successful design technique. The quilt imitates reality: we stand on solid ground and look up at the light sky. Thus it gives solidity to the bottom (grounding the quilt) and gives airiness to the top.

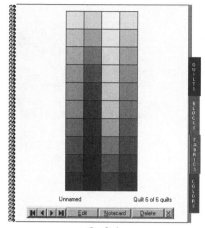

Quilt 1

Let's Play with Value versus Saturation: *Faded Flying Geese*

Value = how light or dark a color is.

Saturation = how pure or grayed a color is.

A grayed version of a pure color is called a tone. Re-read the full description of saturation at the beginning of this lesson, before beginning this quilt, if necessary. We use saturation all the time, but it is one of the hardest concepts to see out of context.

In this quilt, we will play with saturation: pure color versus grayed color. You will use the same four colors you used in Quilts 1 and 2 and the same block: Flying Geese.

Your Flying Geese Gradations quilt should still be on the quilt worktable.

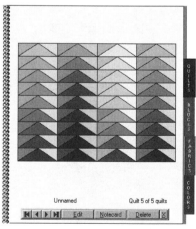

Quilt 2

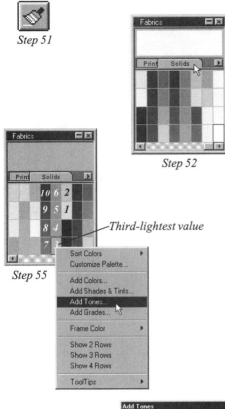

Step 51

Step 52

—*Third-lightest value*

Step 55

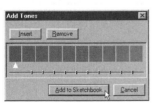

Step 56 - Tones of third-lightest value

Step 59 - Tones of fifth-lightest value

Collect the Tones for *Faded Flying Geese*

Let's choose some variations of the four colors you used. Remember how you created ten values of a color by clicking and then right-clicking on a color? Let's do that again.

51 Click the Paintbrush tool. The Fabrics palette will appear.

52 Click the Solids tab.

53 Scroll to the right end of the Solids palette, where your four value sets await you. Work on one color at a time to avoid confusion.

54 Click the **third-lightest value** of Color 1.

55 Right-click on it and click Add Tones. You will see a range of ten tones from the clear color to gray.

56 Click the Add to Sketchbook button.

57 Scroll to the left and click the **fifth-lightest value** of Color 1.

58 Right-click on it and click Add Tones.

59 Click the Add to Sketchbook button. You now have twenty tones of Color 1 at the far-right end of the palette.

60 Repeat Steps 54 - 59 for the three other colors you are using.

2

Color the Quilt

Work on one column at a time to avoid confusion. Leave the current geese in place. Look at the background triangles. You used only one value in all of those patches. Make sure you are still using the Paintbrush tool.

61 Replace the left side of the background behind every goose with different tones of the color.

62 Generally progress from very gray tones at the top to saturated or more pure colors at the bottom. Remember that you have ten spaces but twenty tones to choose from, so you will not need to use all of them. Experiment by replacing and changing. One side of each goose will be gray and one will remain clear.

63 Repeat Steps 61 - 62 for the three other colors you are using. Notice how the quilt changes as gray is added. It becomes softer and gentler.

64 Click the Save in Sketchbook button when you are finished.

65 If you want, try another version with these or other colors.

66 Save every variation you make in the Sketchbook.

Study and Remember What You Practiced

• Click the View Sketchbook button, then the Quilts tab. Use the arrows to flip through the quilts from beginning to end.

• Notice particularly how the Flying Geese quilts change as tones are added.

• Value and saturation are concepts we know and use all the time. We live with tones, we dress in tones, and we surround ourselves with them in our lives, because the pure and saturated colors are often too strong for anything but small daily doses.

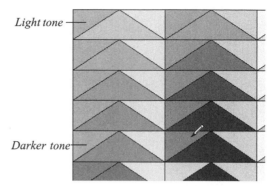

Light tone

Darker tone

Steps 61 - 62

Step 64

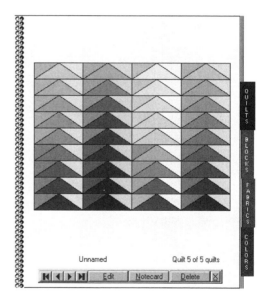

View your quilts in the Sketchbook

2

Where Do Those Tones Come From?

Color Theory

The colors on the color wheel are pure colors. To say it another way, they are the most intense versions of themselves — they are strong and saturated with color, having no gray in them.

We may take any one of these pure colors and change its saturation, thus making it grayer. You practiced this in the Faded Flying Geese quilt. As we add gray to any color, it loses intensity and vibrancy, and becomes a tone of its pure color. Think of the phrase "to tone down"; that's what we do when we gray a color.

Understanding the difference between pure colors, shades, tints, and tones is easier when dealing with solids. When using prints, however, it can sometimes be difficult seeing how you might actually classify a fabric. Is this a tint of red? Is this a light tone of red?

Let's Play with Pure Colors and Their Tones

1 Start EQ5.

2 Choose Create a New Project.

3 Type the name for your new project: C Origin of Tones.

4 Click OK.

5 Click Worktable — Work on Quilt.

Design the Quilt

Layout

6 Click Quilt — New Quilt — Horizontal.

7 Click the Layout tab along the bottom of the screen.

8 Under Number of blocks, click the arrows to read 1 Horizontal and 1 Vertical.

9 Under Size of blocks, drag the sliders to read 12.00 Width and 12.00 Height.

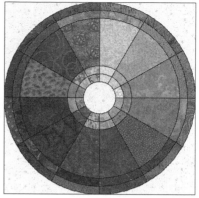

Origin of tones

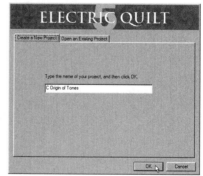

Steps 2-4

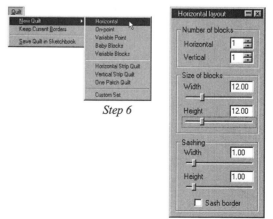

Step 6

Steps 8-9

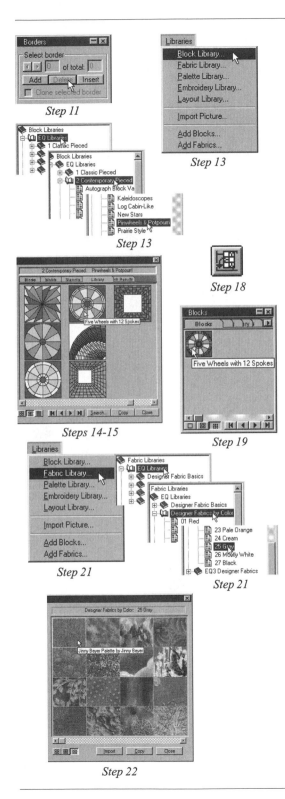

Step 11

Step 13

Step 13

Steps 14-15

Step 18

Step 19

Step 21

Step 21

Step 22

Borders

10 Click the Borders tab along the bottom of the screen.

11 Click the Delete button to eliminate the border.

12 Click the Layer 1 tab along the bottom of the screen.

Blocks

13 Click Libraries — Block Library — EQ Libraries — 2 Contemporary Pieced — Pinwheels & Potpourri. The blocks in this book will appear.

14 Position the cursor over a block and the block name appears. We want the Five Wheels with 12 Spokes block. If your view is still set to 9 blocks at a time, it is the top block in the second-to-last column of this category.

15 Click on the Five Wheels with 12 Spokes block to select it.

16 Click Copy. You'll notice that the block temporarily disappears, indicating you've "copied" it into your Sketchbook.

17 Click Close.

18 Click the Set tool and then the Blocks tab.

19 Click on the Five Wheels block to select it.

20 Click in the center of the quilt.

Collect Your Fabrics

21 Click Libraries — Fabric Library — EQ Libraries — Designer Fabrics By Color — 25 Gray.

22 Copy the **first gray print** from this category.

23 Click Close.

2

24 Now we are going to load 3 palettes from the library, in this order:

- Dried Flower Colors
- Sea and Sky
- Sunrise & Sunset

Repeat Steps 25-27 to load each palette.

25 Click Libraries — Palette Library — EQ5 Palettes.

26 Click on the palette and click Load.

27 Leave it on "Don't delete any fabrics," and click OK.

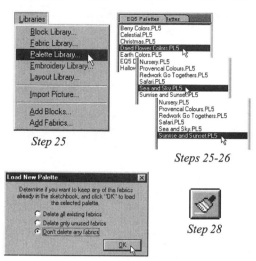

Step 25

Steps 25-26

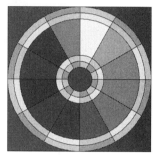

Step 27

Step 28

⟍ Tip

For this lesson, do not sort your prints. We will refer to specific prints and it will be easier if you keep the palettes as they were loaded.

Color the Quilt and Analyze Fabrics

28 Click the Paintbrush tool.

29 Click the Solids tab.

30 Color the twelve large, center pie wedges in the pure colors, starting with yellow in the top-right wedge. Color them in order around the color wheel, using page 17 for reference.

31 Click on the Prints tab.

32 Find a **white or pale neutral print** and click to color all the background of the block (the centermost circle and the 4 corners).

33 Find the single **gray print** you copied from the Fabric library.

34 Click to color all twelve patches just *outside* of the large pie wedges. It will look like a gray ring around the color wheel.

35 Find the **light gray print** from the Hannah's Garden line by Robyn Pandolph in the Sea and Sky palette.

36 Click to color all twelve patches just *inside* of the large pie wedges.

Step 30

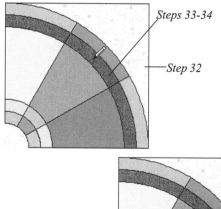

Steps 33-34

Step 32

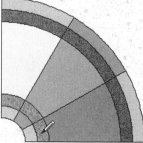

Step 36

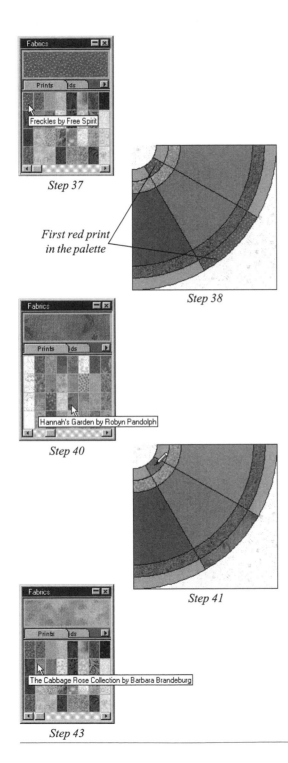

Step 37

First red print in the palette

Step 38

Step 40

Step 41

Step 43

Now you should see a dark and a light gray ring on either side of your color wheel. Let's color the innermost and outermost rings with prints.

For each wedge, fill the inner and outer sections of each wedge with grayed tones of the pure colors. It is harder to pinpoint the color relationship with prints than with solids, so this lesson is an important exercise for your color sense. You can always change the fabrics around and see how the colors look.

37 Click the **first red print in the EQ5 palette** (red with tiny yellow dots).

38 Find red on your wheel and click this into the patches outside of your dark gray and light gray.

Does this red print seem like you could mix the solid red and dark gray to get this fabric? What about with the light gray? Hopefully you answered "no" to both questions. This red print looks more pure than like a red tone.

39 Scroll in the Fabrics palette to see the Dried Flower Colors palette.

40 Find and click on the **dark rose print** from the Hannah's Garden line by Robyn Pandolph. (It is the third and darkest rose print in the Dried Flower Colors palette.)

41 Click this print into the outermost and innermost rings of the red wedge to replace your pure print.

Ask yourself these questions; can I mix solid red with either of the gray bands and get this fabric? Perhaps you can on the outer ring, but not the inner one. Let's leave the dark rose print in the outside, but find a new one for the inside.

42 Scroll in the Fabrics palette to see the beginning of the EQ5 palette.

43 Find and click on the **pink fabric** named The Cabbage Rose Collection by Barbara Brandeburg.

2

44 Click this into the innermost ring of the red wedge.

Does this print look like it comes from solid red and light gray? No, it looks more like a red tint than a light red tone.

45 Scroll in the Fabrics palette to see the Dried Flower Colors palette.

46 Find the **first rose print** from the Folk Art Wedding line by Robyn Pandolph.

2

47 Click this into the innermost ring of the red wedge.

Now you've found two prints that are red tones. How about trying this for the rest of the wheel?

I suggest this as a method: Scroll through the palette and stop on grayed tones (ignore the bright, pure colors). Try to decide where each fabric came from and click it into a space. As you go through analyzing each fabric, replace old prints with better examples.

48 Continue around the wheel and find two tones for each color. If you think you don't have enough fabrics, go to the Libraries — Fabric Library — EQ Libraries — Designer Fabric Basics or Designer Fabrics by Color and copy more.

49 Click the Save in Sketchbook button.

Color Your Quilt Competely With Prints

Now that you understand that tones come from adding gray to pure colors, let's get rid of those gray rings.

50 Find and click in other **tones of pure colors** on top of your gray patches. You should now have four tones for each solid color on the wheel.

51 Find the **first pure red print** you used in Step 38 and color this on top the large solid red.

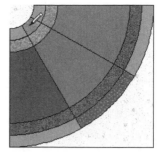

Step 44

Step 46

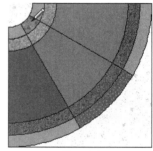

Step 47

Step 49

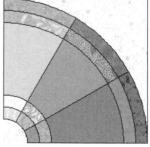

Step 50

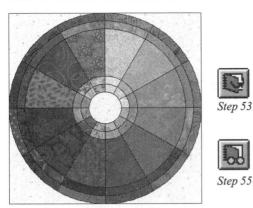

Step 52

Step 53

Step 55

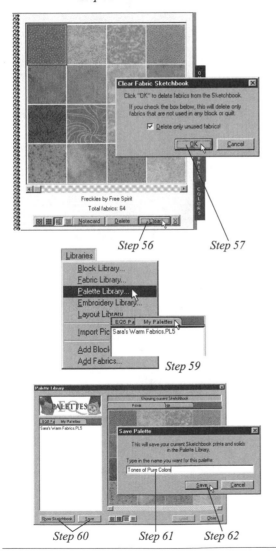

Step 56

Step 57

Step 59

Step 60   *Step 61*   *Step 62*

52 Find **other pure-colored prints** to replace the solids on the wheel.

53 Click Save in Sketchbook when you're finished.

54 Make another version if you want to and save it in your Sketchbook. One should be enough and should take quite a bit of time.

Save Your Current Fabrics as a Palette in the Library

55 Click the View Sketchbook button, then the Fabrics tab.

56 Click the Clear button.

57 Click OK (making sure to leave the check next to "Delete only unused fabrics").

58 Click the X in the bottom-right corner of the Sketchbook.

59 Click Libraries — Palette Library — My Palettes tab (behind the EQ5 Palettes tab).

60 Click the Show Sketchbook button then click Save.

61 Type: Tones of Pure Colors

62 Press ENTER on your keyboard or click Save.

63 Click Close to put away the Palette Library.

Study your Quilt and Remember What You Practiced

- Sit back and stare at the quilt or click View the Sketchbook button and use the arrows to find what you consider the best quilt and stare at it.

- Remember how hard it is to see the relationship of a pure color and its tones in prints.

- But remember, too, where the tones come from and how they come to exist.

2

How Much Chroma?

Color Theory

Chroma is the Greek root meaning *color*. It is a useful term because it allows us to use and understand the words below, which are derived from it.

Achromatic

A means *without*, so an *achromatic* color scheme is one without color, usually a neutral color scheme of black, white and gray.

2

Monochromatic

Mono means *one*, so a *monochromatic* color scheme is a one-color color scheme. It can contain many values of the one color. This is a popular color scheme in quilting because it is easy to do and always successful. It is thus good for beginners.

Polychromatic

Poly means *many*, so a *polychromatic* color scheme is one that uses many colors together. Although we rarely use the term *polychromatic*, we use the color scheme all the time.

Finished Monochromatic Quilt

Let's Play with Chroma.

1   Start EQ5.

2   Choose Create a New Project.

3   Type the name for your new project: C Chroma - Texas Tears.

4   Click OK.

5   Click Worktable — Work on Quilt.

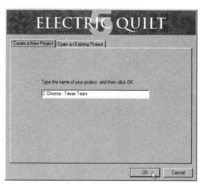

Steps 2-4

Step 5

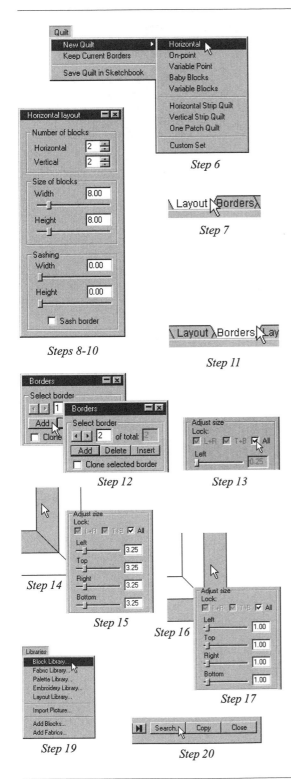

Step 6

Step 7

Steps 8-10

Step 11

Step 12

Step 13

Step 14

Step 15

Step 16

Step 17

Step 19

Step 20

Design the Chroma Quilt

Layout

6 Click Quilt — New Quilt — Horizontal.

7 Click the Layout tab along the bottom of the screen.

8 Under Number of blocks, click the arrows to read 2 Horizontal and 2 Vertical.

9 Under Size of blocks, drag the sliders to read 8.00 Width and 8.00 Height.

10 Under Sashing, drag both sliders to read 0.00 to eliminate the sashing.

Borders

11 Click the Borders tab along the bottom of the screen.

12 Click the Add button once so you have a total of 2 borders.

13 Be sure there is a check next to All under Adjust Size. (Clicking will turn this check on and off.)

14 Click the inner border.

15 Drag one of the sliders to make it 3.25. All sides will adjust automatically.

16 Click the outer border.

17 Drag one of the sliders to 1.00. All sides will adjust automatically.

18 Click the Layer 1 tab along the bottom of the screen.

Block

19 Click Libraries — Block Library on the top menu bar.

20 Click the Search button.

2

21 Make sure there is a check next to "Search Name."

22 Type the word "Texas" without quotes.

23 Click the Search button on this box.

24 When the results message pops up, click OK. We want the Texas Tears block.

25 Place your cursor over a block without clicking and the block name appears. Click on the Texas Tears block to select it.

26 Click Copy. The block temporarily disappears, indicating you've copied it into your Sketchbook.

27 Click Close.

28 Click the Set tool. Click the Blocks tab, then the Texas Tears block so it is selected.

29 Position your cursor over any block space in the center of your empty quilt layout. Hold down your keyboard CTRL key and click. Your quilt is now filled with four blocks.

Collect the Fabrics for your Achromatic Quilt

30 Click the View Sketchbook button, then click the Fabrics tab.

These are the "default" fabrics in EQ5 that every new project starts with. We're going to use our own fabrics from the Fabric Library, so let's remove these extra fabrics.

31 Click the Clear button.

32 Click OK. All the fabrics in the Sketchbook will disappear. Now let's add our own.

33 Click the X in the bottom-right corner to close the Sketchbook.

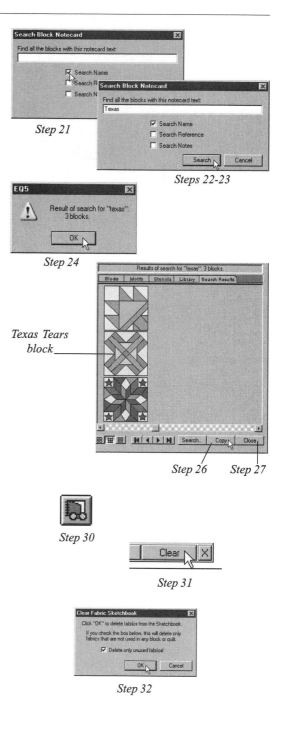

Step 21

Steps 22-23

Step 24

Texas Tears block

Step 26   Step 27

Step 30

Step 31

Step 32

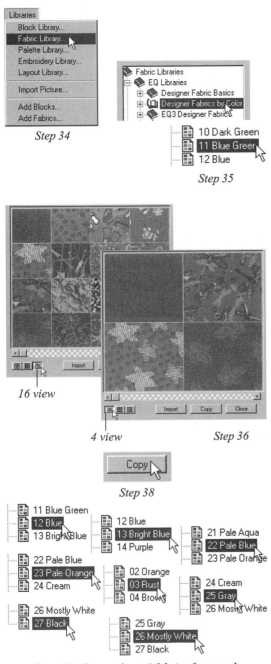

Step 34

Step 35

16 view

4 view   *Step 36*

Step 38

Step 41 - Copy at least 6 fabrics from each.

Step 42

34 Click Libraries – Fabric Library – EQ Libraries – Designer Fabrics by Color. You will choose six fabrics from each of the books listed below. Include a variety of prints and pattern. The process is simple. Let's try it.

35 Click on 11 Blue Green.

36 Scroll through the fabric swatches to view your choices. Notice the three buttons below the Style box. They contain 4, 9, or 16 squares and control how many swatches you can see at the same time. Change your view to 16 to see as many as possible. Change your view to 4 to get a close-up of a fabric's pattern.

37 Choose any fabric in 11 Blue Green, and click on it.

38 Click Copy.

39 Find another fabric in this category, click on it and click Copy.

40 Repeat this for a total of at least six fabrics from this category.

Tip

You can copy *all the fabrics in a style* quickly with the ENTER key. Just click the first fabric to select it, click the Copy button once, then hold down the ENTER key on your keyboard until all the fabrics disappear indicating they've been sent to your Sketchbook. (This tip works with the Block, Fabric, and Layout libraries as well as with the Delete button in the Sketchbook.)

41 Repeat Steps 36 – 40 for each of these other categories (in this order):

12 Blue	03 Rust
13 Bright Blue	25 Gray
22 Pale Blue	27 Black
23 Pale Orange	26 Mostly White

42 Click Close. You are back to the quilt worktable.

43 Click the Swap tool (not the EQ4 swap tool), then click on the Prints tab at the top of the palette.

Step 43

44 Scroll through the fabrics to see your choices.

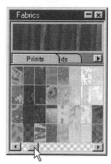

Step 44

Color the Achromatic Quilt

You will design at least three quilts: an achromatic, a monochromatic and a polychromatic one. I strongly suggest you design and save more than one of each kind.

The first quilt will be an achromatic quilt. Remember, achromatic means colorless, so in your achromatic quilt you have no colors to work with. We will try for variety and contrast using what you DO have: a full range of dark and light values and textured prints.

Save several versions

45 Find a **white** print in the palette and click to select it.

46 Click on the small on-point square in the center of one of your Texas Tears blocks. Your white fabric will replace the lilac color everywhere in the quilt: in the outer X and in the on-point squares.

✎ **Tip** _____

If you make a mistake while coloring, choose Edit — Undo from the menu bar at the top of your screen, or press CTRL + Z on your keyboard.

47 Find and click on a **gray** print in the palette.

48 Click on the inner, pink X in your Texas Tears block. The pink will be replaced by gray.

49 Find and click on a **medium-value black** or a **dark gray** print.

50 Click to replace the beige background of the Texas Tears blocks in your quilt.

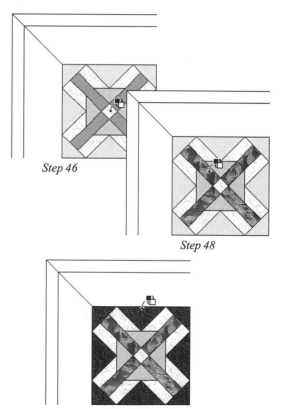

Step 46

Step 48

Step 50

Step 51

Step 52

Steps 54-56

51 Find and click on a **dark-value black** print. Click on a golden-yellow triangle in the center of one of your blocks.

52 You have finished the center of your first achromatic quilt. Click the Save in Sketchbook button.

53 Optional: Try more achromatic quilt centers: put black, gray and white in different placements each time. Save any versions you like in your Sketchbook.

Color the Border

Now, let's color the border to see how it can affect the center design. With each change, alter both the inner and outer border. There are many options. Try the ones below and a few others you might think of. Don't forget to save each change in the Sketchbook.

54 Try different combinations of two fabrics you used in the center blocks. Save the quilt in your Sketchbook.

55 Try one light and one dark border. Reverse the values and see how the overall look changes. Save the quilt in your Sketchbook.

56 Try busy prints and then change to simpler ones. Save the quilt in your Sketchbook.

57 Optional: Try Steps 54-56 for any of your other achromatic quilt centers.

Study your Achromatic Quilts

- Click the View Sketchbook button, then the Quilts tab. Use the arrows to flip through a slide show of the different versions of the Achromatic Quilt.

- Notice how and when value affects which part of the block you see first.

- Notice how the color of the borders also has an affect on which elements stand out. This is because of proportion: a large quantity of one fabric or value makes it stronger in relation to others.

2

Color the Monochromatic Quilt

The second quilt will be a monochromatic quilt.
Remember, monochromatic means one color, so
in your monochromatic quilt you have only one
color to work with. You must try for variety and
contrast using what you DO have: a full range
of dark and light values and textured prints.

58 For your Monochromatic Quilt, follow
Steps 45-57, using **values of blue** instead of
blacks, grays and whites.

59 Save any of the quilts you like in the
Sketchbook.

Tip

**You can use your achromatic quilts as a
starting point. Click the View Sketchbook
button and then the Quilts tab. Use the arrows
to find one of your achromatic quilts. When
you find one you like, click the Edit button.
You will now have that quilt on the worktable.
Use the Swap tool to change your blacks,
grays and whites to blue values.**

Study your Monochromatic Quilts & Remember What You Learned

• Click the View Sketchbook button and then
the Quilts tab. Use the arrows to flip
through a slide show of the different
versions of the Monochromatic Quilt.

• Notice what parts of the blocks stand out
and how different borders affect the design.

Color a Polychromatic Quilt

The third quilt will be a polychromatic quilt.
Remember, polychromatic means many colors,
so in your polychromatic quilt you have at least
two colors to work with. You will find it easier to
get variety and contrast. DO include a full range
of dark and light values.

60 For your Polychromatic Quilts, follow Steps
45-57, using blues, blue-greens, rusts, and
pale oranges instead of gray, black or white.

61 Save any of the quilts you like in your
Sketchbook.

Monochromatic Quilts

Step 59

Polychromatic Quilts

Step 61

Study your Polychromatic Quilts

Study All of your Quilts & Remember What You Learned

- Click the View Sketchbook button and then the Quilts tab. Use the arrows to flip through a slide show of the different versions of the three color schemes. In the first two sets — achromatic and monochromatic — you only had different values and texture to provide variety and contrast. In the last set, when you were allowed more colors, you had an easier task.

- Notice how and when value affects what part of the block stands out.

- In your Polychromatic Quilts, see if you can decide which colors stand out the most. We will learn more about this in the "How Colors Behave" chapter.

- Notice how the borders also change which elements stand out. This is because of proportion: a large quantity of one fabric or value makes it stronger in relation to others.

2

Color Harmony and Contrast

Chapter 3

Complementary Colors are Opposites

Color Theory

For every color there is a complement. It is the color directly opposite that color on the color wheel. Notice that the complement of yellow is violet, of red is green, and so on. To complement something means to finish it (not compliment, which is what we hope to receive when we have finished our quilts). When a complement finishes a color, it creates harmony, which is more pleasing to the eye.

Since two complements always go together, they make a perfect and powerful color scheme.

Remember, complements are exact opposites. If they are used together equally, they vibrate and hurt the eye. The trick to using complements together is to use them unequally.

Let's Play with Complements

1. Start EQ5.

2. Choose Create a New Project.

3. Type the name for your new project: C Complementary Colors - Suns.

4. Click OK.

5. Click Worktable — Work on Quilt.

Chart the Complementary Pairs

Layout

6. Click Quilt — New Quilt — Horizontal.

7. Click the Layout tab along the bottom of the screen.

8. Under Number of blocks, click the arrows to read 10 Horizontal and 6 Vertical.

9. Under Size of blocks, drag the sliders to read 6.00 Width and 6.00 Height.

10. Under Sashing, drag the sliders to read 0.00 Width and 0.75 Height. Be sure Sash border is *not* checked. (Clicking here will turn this check on and off.)

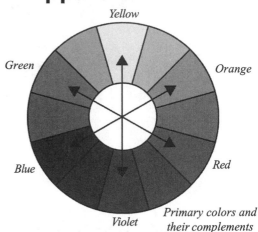

Primary colors and their complements

Steps 2-4

Step 6

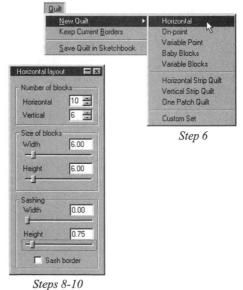
Steps 8-10

Step 12

Step 14

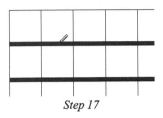
Step 17

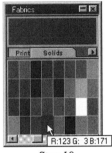
Step 18

1	2	3	4	5

Step 19

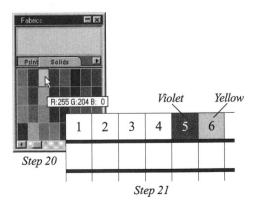

Violet *Yellow*

1	2	3	4	5	6

Step 20

Step 21

Borders

11 Click the Borders tab along the bottom of the screen.

12 Click the Delete button to eliminate all borders.

13 Click the Layer 1 tab along the bottom of the screen.

Color the Chart with Pairs of Complements

14 Click the Paintbrush tool.

15 Click the Solids tab on the palette.

16 Scroll to find **black** and click it to select it.

17 Hold down the CTRL key on your keyboard and click in the horizontal sashing. These black bands will divide your complementary pairs from each other. Look at the Color wheel on page 17. Go around the wheel clockwise and find the pairs of complements.

You will insert the six pairs of complements into your chart's center two columns, beginning at the top and working downward. Use the pure versions of each color. Refer to the color wheel to match them.

18 Find **pure violet** in the palette and click to select it.

19 Click on the top square in the 5th column.

20 Find **pure yellow** in the palette and click on it to select it.

21 Click on the top square in 6th column to make it yellow. You now have a pair of complements.

3

22 Follow Steps 18-21, placing the complementary pairs in order from top to bottom, placing the cool colors in the 5th column and the warm colors in the 6th column.

Violet and yellow

Blue-violet and yellow-orange

Blue and orange

Blue-green and red-orange

Green and red

Yellow-green and red-violet

23 Save this Complementary Colors Chart in the Sketchbook.

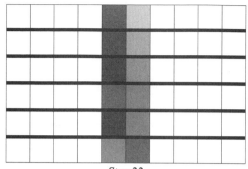

Step 22

You now have a chart of the six pairs of complements or complementary colors. Take a moment to study the complementary pairs of pure colors. Remember three important things about them:

Step 23   *Step 24*

- They are guaranteed to go together.

- Because they are opposites, they always make a powerful color scheme.

- They can be used unequally to offset their strong contrast.

Add Shades & Tints for Each Color

Now we need to add shades and tints for every color in our color wheel.

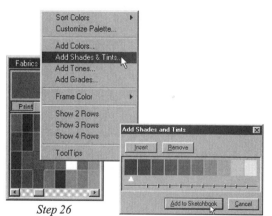

Step 26

Step 27

24 Click the Eyedropper tool.

25 Click on **violet** in your chart. The Eyedropper will pick up violet in the palette.

26 Right-click on top of violet in the palette and choose Add Shades & Tints.

27 Click Add to Sketchbook. The ten added values are at the end of your palette.

28 Click the Eyedropper tool and pick up **blue-violet** in your quilt.

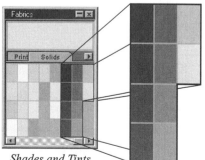

Shades and Tints are displayed at the end of your palette

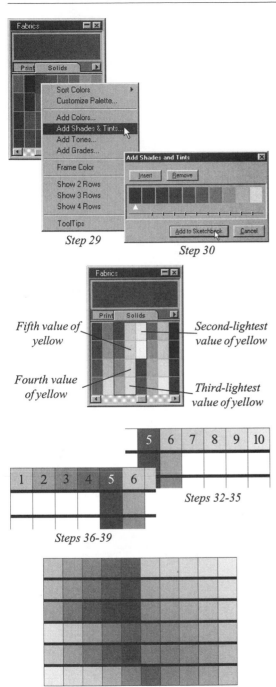

Step 29

Step 30

Fifth value of yellow

Second-lightest value of yellow

Fourth value of yellow

Third-lightest value of yellow

Steps 32-35

Steps 36-39

Finished Complementary Chart

Step 41

29 Right-click on top of blue-violet in the palette and choose Add Shades & Tints.

30 Click Add to Sketchbook.

31 Repeat Steps 28-30 for the rest of the colors in column five and then also for column six.

Add Four Values of Each Color

Scroll to the right end of the palette and see the sets of Shades and Tints you added. There are ten values of each color. For this lesson, ignore the lightest and the darkest values and choose from the middle values.

32 You are now going to add four values to the side of each color. Find the shades and tints of yellow. Click the **second-lightest value of yellow**. Click to place it in the 10th column of the first row.

33 Click the **third-lightest value of yellow** and place it in the 9th column of the first row.

34 Click the **fourth value of yellow** and place it in the 8th column of the first row.

35 Click the **fifth value of yellow** and place it in the 7th column next to pure yellow.

36 Find the shades and tints of violet. Click the **second-lightest value of violet**. Click to place it in the 1st column of the first row.

37 Click the **third-lightest value of violet** and place it in the 2nd column of the first row.

38 Click the **fourth value of violet** and click to place it in the 3rd column.

39 Click the **fifth value of violet**. Click to place it next to pure violet in the 4th column.

40 Repeat Steps 32-39 for the remaining pairs of complements.

41 Save the completed chart in the Sketchbook.

3

Take a moment to look again at the six pairs of complements. You now have four values of each complement. **Just as the complements are guaranteed to go together, so are all of their values.**

Gather Prints to Make Your Own Palette

Throughout this book we will be working with the twelve colors of the color wheel and their shades, tints, and tones. We already made a Tones palette when we did the Origin of Tones lesson. Let's make a palette of pure colors and their values and save it for later use.

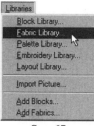

Step 67

42 Click Libraries — Fabric Library — EQ Libraries. Notice some of the categories listed. We will focus on Designer Fabric Basics and Designer Fabrics by Color, but use any of the EQ4 Novelties or EQ4 Textures by Color if necessary.

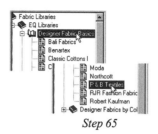

Step 65

43 Click Designer Fabrics Basics — P & B Textiles.

44 Copy at least five prints that are **violet** in color. We need a variety of values, so try to find at least three pure violets, one shade and one tint. Be sure to get a variety of textures and patterns. You may also look in Robert Kaufman and Classic Cottons II until you've copied at least five.

Step 66

45 Click Close.

46 Click the Paintbrush tool, then the Prints tab.

Step 63

47 Find a **violet tint** you copied from the Library and click it into the left square of row one.

48 Click **three different pure violets** into squares two, three and four of row one. You may also use one or two violets from the default EQ5 palette.

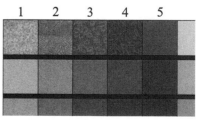

Step 54

Add the violet shade

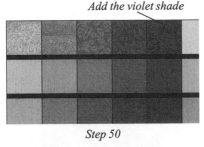

Step 50

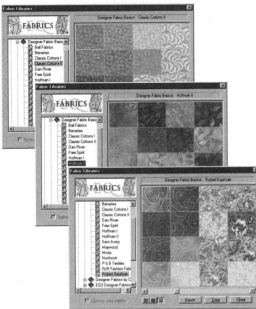

Fabric libraries with great values, tints and shades can be found in any of these catagories

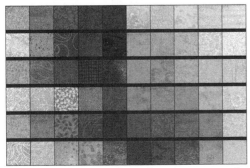

Your final fabric chart of pure colors, tints and shades

Step 52

49 Compare the three pure violet prints with your solid violet in column five. If they do not seem to go well together, replace the prints with others you collected or go to the Fabric Library to get more.

50 Find a **violet shade** in your palette. Click in your chart to replace the solid violet of column five with this dark print.

51 Repeat Steps 42-50 for the other pure colors. Do one color at a time. Remember to find **three pure prints, one shade and one tint**. Here are the colors yet to do and where you might find their prints:

Blue-violet — 12 Blue, Moda, P & B Textiles, Classic Cottons I (tints)

Blue — Classic Cottons I, Classic Cottons II, Maywood (shade)

Blue-green — 11 Blue Green, Classic Cottons II (shades & tints)

Green — 08 Green, Classic Cottons II (shades & tints), P & B Textiles (tints)

Yellow-green — 07 Yellow Green, Classic Cottons II (tints)

Yellow — 06 Yellow, Maywood (tints), P & B Textiles (tints)

Yellow-orange — Northcott (shades & pure), Classic Cottons I (pure & tints), Hoffman II (pure at very end)

Orange — 02 Orange (do not get red-orange prints), P & B Textiles, Classic Cottons I (tints)

Red-orange — 02 Orange (get only red-orange prints), 01 Red (red-orange plaid), Robert Kaufman (pure), P & B Textiles (tints)

Red — 01 Red, P & B Textiles (tints)

Red-violet — RJR Fashion Fabrics (shades), 16 Magenta, Classic Cottons II (tints)

52 Click Save in Sketchbook to keep this final chart of prints.

3

Make Your Own Palette

We only need the sixty prints in this quilt for our palette, so let's delete the unused prints.

53 Click the View Sketchbook button, then the Fabrics tab.

54 Click the Clear button.

55 Just click OK (making sure to leave the check next to "Delete only unused fabrics").

56 Click the X in the bottom-right corner of the Sketchbook.

57 Click Libraries — Palette Library — My Palettes tab (behind the EQ5 Palettes tab).

58 Click the Show Sketchbook button then click Save.

59 Type: Pure Colors and Values

60 Press ENTER on your keyboard or click Save.

61 Click Close to put away the Palette Library.

Let's Design a Quilt: The Setting Sun

Layout

62 Click Quilt — New Quilt — Horizontal.

63 Click the Layout tab along the bottom of the screen.

64 Under Number of blocks, click the arrows to read 3 Horizontal and 3 Vertical.

65 Under Size of blocks, drag the sliders to read 14.00 Width and 14.00 Height.

66 Under Sashing, drag the sliders to read 1.00 Width and 1.00 Height. Be sure there is a check next to Sash border.

Borders

67 Click the Borders tab.

68 Under Select border, click the Add button twice to make a total of three borders.

Step 53   *Step 54*

Step 55

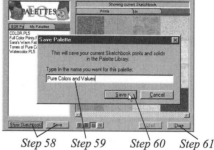

Step 58   *Step 59*   *Step 60*   *Step 61*

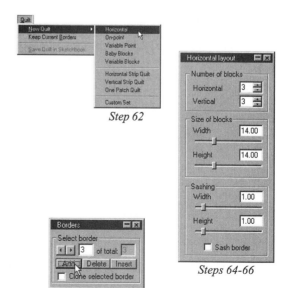

Step 62

Steps 64-66

Step 68

3

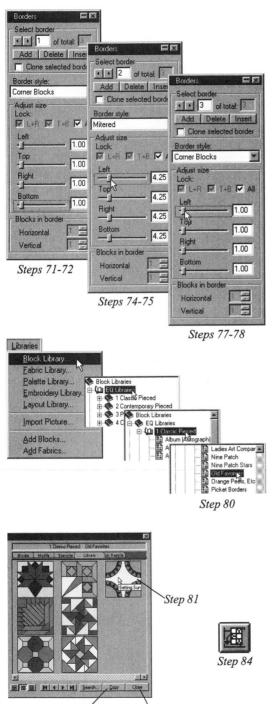

Steps 71-72

Steps 74-75

Steps 77-78

Step 80

Step 81

Step 84

Step 82   *Step 83*

69 Be sure there is a check next to All under Adjust size. (Clicking will turn this check on and off.)

70 Click on the inner border.

71 Under Border style, click the dropdown arrow and choose Corner Blocks.

72 Drag one of the sliders to 1.00. All sides will adjust automatically.

73 Click on the middle border.

74 Under Border style, choose Mitered.

75 Drag one of the sliders to read 4.25.

76 Click on the outer border.

77 Under Border style, choose Corner Blocks.

78 Drag one of the sliders to read 1.00.

Layer 1

79 Click the Layer 1 tab.

80 Click Libraries — Block Library — EQ Libraries — 1 Classic Pieced — Old Favorites.

81 Find and click on the Setting Sun block to select it. (It is the last block in the Old Favorites category.)

82 Click the Copy button. You'll notice the block temporarily disappears, indicating you've copied it to your Sketchbook.

83 Click Close.

84 Click the Set tool and then the Blocks tab.

85 Click on the Setting Sun block in the palette.

86 Hold down your keyboard CTRL key and click on the quilt center to fill all the squares with the Setting Sun block.

3

Let's Color Six Quilts in Complementary Color Schemes

Look at the design you have created: suns divided by or perhaps trapped behind the window-like sashing strips. You will treat the inner border as part of the sashing design, and use prints in a variety of values and tones for the quilts.

Step 87

87 Click the Swap tool (not the EQ4 Swap tool).

88 Click the Prints tab.

89 Find a **pure violet** print and click to select it.

90 Click on the large cream-colored center of one block in the quilt to change all centers to violet. These pieces will become the background.

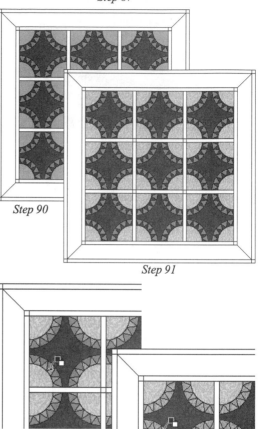

Step 90

Step 91

91 Choose a **pure yellow** print from the palette. Click in a quarter-circle corner of one block. All corners of all blocks will color at the same time.

92 Choose a **second yellow** print to recolor the brown points of the suns. Click on an outward-pointing triangle in one block to color the points of all the blocks at the same time.

93 Choose a **light violet** from the palette and click to recolor all the dark orange triangles outside the points of one sun. The triangles outside all of the suns will color at the same time. These will be background.

Step 92

Step 93

94 Click the Paintbrush tool.

Step 94

95 Find a **third contrasting pure yellow** print. Hold down your keyboard CTRL key and click in two of the quarter-circle corners of one block: the bottom-left and the top-right. All these corners will color at the same time.

96 Choose a **medium violet** from the palette and CTRL + click to color the sashing, inner border, and outer border.

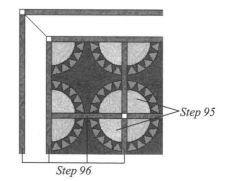

→*Step 95*

Step 96

Step 97

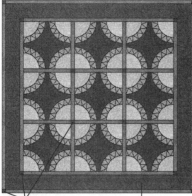

Step 99   *Step 100*

Step 101

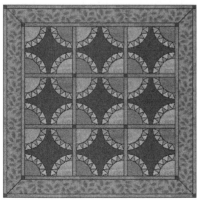

Step 102

Step 103

97 Click the Eyedropper tool.

98 Click on the **pure violet** print in the quilt that you used as the large background for the suns. The eyedropper will pick up the color and switch you automatically back to the Paintbrush tool.

99 CTRL + click to color the tiny squares (called cornerstones) in the sashing as well as the squares in the inner and outer borders.

100 Find and click on a **contrasting medium violet** and CTRL + click to place it in the middle border. You now have a quilt in a complementary color scheme, which includes several fabrics and values of each color.

101 Click the Save in Sketchbook button.

102 Using the Swap tool or CTRL + click with the Paintbrush tool, create a different version of the violet and yellow complementary quilt. The first Setting Sun quilt contained more violet than yellow. Create a predominantly yellow quilt.

103 Save Quilt 2 in the Sketchbook.

104 Repeat Steps 87-101 to make quilts in each of the other pairs of complementary colors. Follow these coloring rules:

- Make one quilt at a time, using two complements in each.

- Make the quilts in the color order used for the chart at the beginning of this lesson, referring to the samples.

- Play with vivid colors and prints.

- Include a variety of values and tones.

- Use the complements UNEQUALLY.

3

- Try different border combinations (by varying the values), but use both complements in the border design.

- Make two or more quilts in every complementary pair of colors. Make them different from each other by changing fabrics and the proportion of the two colors.

- Save all the quilts you make in the Sketchbook.

Study Your Setting Sun Complementary Quilts

- Click the View Sketchbook button and then the Quilts tab. Use the arrows to flip through a slide show of the complement charts and the different versions of your Setting Sun Complementary Quilt.

- In the Setting Sun, notice how the quilt's design changes depending on where you put the pure colors, tints and shades.

- In the Setting Sun, notice also how the borders affect the designs. Some borders are probably stronger compared to the center of the quilt, whereas others might look too weak.

Remember

- All values of a color are complementary with those of its complement.

- You can use complements unequally for color balance.

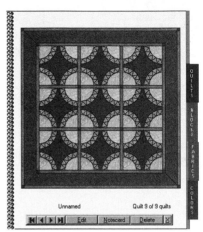

Flip through your Sketchbook to view your quilts and to refer to the complementary charts you made at the beginning of this lesson.

3

3

Analogous Colors are Neighbors

Color Theory

Analogous colors are ones right next to each other on the color wheel. Analogous colors always go together because they are so closely related. You can't go wrong combining them. Any quilt based on analogous colors is bound to have movement and contrast.

Let's Play with Analogous Colors

1   Start EQ5.

2   Choose Create a New Project.

3   Type the name for your new project:
     C Analogous Colors - Swirls.

4   Click OK.

Design a Block

5   Click Worktable — Work on Block.

6   Click Libraries — Block Library — EQ Libraries — 2 Contemporary Pieced — Pinwheels & Potpourri.

7   Drag the horizontal scrollbar below the block to the right to see all the blocks in this book.

8   You want the Nine Degree Wedge block in the last column. Position the cursor over a block and the block name appears. This will help you find the block.

9   Click on the Nine Degree Wedge block to select it. You'll see a frame around it to know it's the selected one.

10 Click Copy. You'll notice that the block temporarily disappears, indicating you've "copied" it into your Sketchbook.

11 Click Close.

Steps 2-4

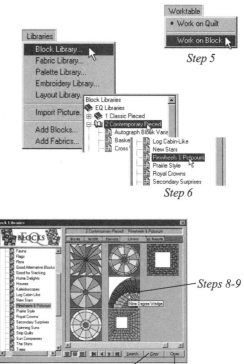

Step 5

Step 6

Steps 8-9

Step 10   Step 11

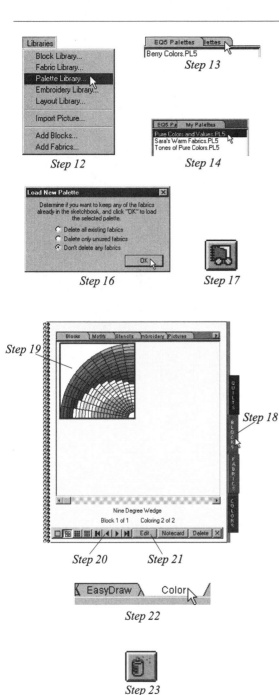

Step 12

Step 13

Step 14

Step 16

Step 17

Step 19

Step 18

Step 20   Step 21

Step 22

Step 23

Collect the Fabrics for the Quilt

12 Click Libraries — Palette Library.

13 Click on the My Palettes tab behind the EQ5 Palettes tab.

14 Click on the Pure Colors and Values palette.

15 Click the Load button. A message will pop up, asking what to do with the current fabric palette.

16 Click "Don't delete any fabrics," then OK.

Edit the Block to the Worktable

17 Click the View Sketchbook button.

18 On the right side of the sketchbook, click the Blocks tab.

19 Click on the Nine Degree Wedge block.

20 Use the colorway arrows to click backward one coloring to the grayscale version of this block.

21 Click the Edit button. You will now be on the Block Worktable.

Color the Block

22 Click the Color tab along the bottom of your screen. You are going to play with prints by changing these grays to a set of 3-4 analogous colors. Begin with red-violet, violet, blue-violet and blue. Use several values of each color to add contrast.

23 To make coloring easy, you will use the Spraycan tool on the right toolbar. Click the Spraycan tool to view the fabrics.

✎ Tip _____

Be sure you use the Spraycan tool, not the EQ4 Spraycan, because it will cause a totally different effect than you are looking for.

3

24 Click the Prints tab on the palette. Scroll through the swatches to see the array of fabrics available for your quilt.

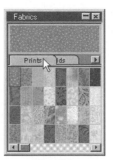

Step 24

25 To use the Spraycan, click on the fabric you want to use from the palette, then click on any patch in the block. All patches in that previous color are changed to the new selected color.

26 Begin at the center of the block and place red-violet there. Work outward, using the colors in order from red-violet through blue. Use several values (light, pure, dark) of each.

27 When you finish, sit back and look at the block. Change any values or colors you want to. If there is too much of any color, click on a different fabric in the palette, and click on that overpowering color with the Spraycan. Wherever that color was in the block, it will be replaced by the new color.

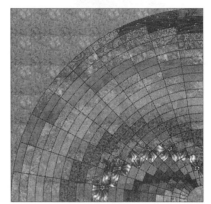

Steps 25-27

28 Click the Save in Sketchbook button when you are happy with the way the block is colored.

Steps 28

Color Blocks 2 and 3 in Different Analogous Color Combinations

29 Repeat Steps 23-28 to color and save two more blocks, each in a different analogous colors set:

- Block 2: yellow, yellow-orange, orange, red-orange and red

- Block 3: blue, blue-green, green and yellow-green

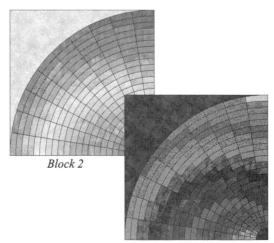

Block 2

Block 3

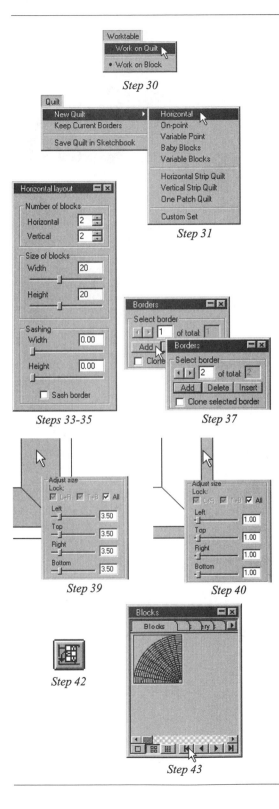

Step 30

Step 31

Steps 33-35

Step 37

Step 39

Step 40

Step 42

Step 43

Setup the Quilt

Layout

30 Click Worktable — Work on Quilt. You will now be back to the Quilt Worktable.

31 Click Quilt — New Quilt — Horizontal.

32 Click the Layout tab along the bottom of the screen.

33 Under Number of blocks, click the arrows to read 2 Horizontal and 2 Vertical.

34 Under Size of blocks, drag the sliders to read 20.00 Width and 20.00 Height.

35 Under Sashing, drag both sliders to read 0.00.

Border

36 Click the Borders tab along the bottom of the screen.

37 Click the Add button once to make a total of 2 borders.

38 Be sure there is a check next to All under Adjust Size. (Clicking will turn this check on and off.)

39 Click on the inner border. Drag one of the sliders to 3.50. All borders will adjust automatically.

40 Click on the outer border. Drag one of the sliders to read 1.00. All borders will adjust automatically.

41 Click the Layer 1 tab along the bottom of the screen.

Design the Quilt

42 Click the Set tool. The Nine Degree Wedge block is there, and your colorings are stacked behind one another.

43 Click the first colorway arrow to go to the line drawing version of the block.

3

44 Click the third colorway arrow a total of 3 times to go to the grayscale version, then the library's colored version, and finally your first coloring.

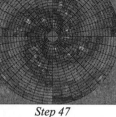

Step 44 -
Click 3 times

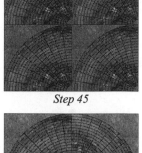

Step 45

45 Hold down the CTRL key on your keyboard and click in one square on your quilt. All squares will fill with a fully colored Nine Degree Wedge.

46 Click the Rotate tool.

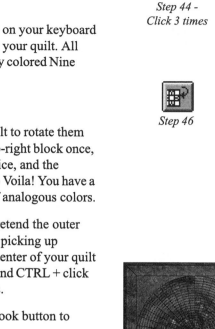

Step 46

47 Click the blocks in the quilt to rotate them into a circle. (Click the top-right block once, the bottom-right block twice, and the bottom-left block 3 times.) Voila! You have a full circle in gradations of analogous colors.

Step 47

48 Now color the borders. Pretend the outer border is the binding. Try picking up different colors from the center of your quilt with the Eyedropper tool and CTRL + click to use them in the borders.

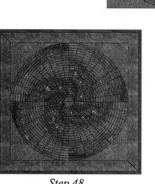

Step 49

49 Click the Save in Sketchbook button to save some quilts you like.

Step 50

Make Two More Swirling Analogous Colors Quilts

50 Keep the same quilt layout. Click the Set tool.

Step 48

Step 51 -
Click 1 time

51 Click the third colorway arrow one time to go to the next analogous coloring you made.

52 Hold down the CTRL key on your keyboard and click on top of the blocks already there to replace them with this coloring.

53 Follow Steps 48-49 to make several versions of the second coloration.

54 Keep the same quilt layout and follow Steps 50-53 for Block 3 with its different coloration.

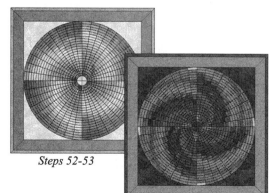

Steps 52-53

Step 54

3

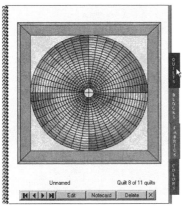

Study Your Quilts

Study Your Analogous Quilts and Remember What You Practiced

- Click the View Sketchbook button, then click the Quilts tab.

- Use the arrows on the Sketchbook to flip through a slide show of the different versions of your Swirling Analogous Colors quilts.

- Notice which colors stand out and which recede.

- Notice how changing the border color affects which colors stand out. This happens when you add a lot of one color, making it stronger in relation to other colors.

Remember

- Analogous colors always work well together because they are close cousins.

- Analogous colors create movement, too, for the same reason.

3

Practice with Value in Floating Fans

Color Theory

Value is an important concept to understand in quilt design. It can add variety, interest, and even illusion. In this lesson we are going to use pinwheel-like fans on a black background to show how value gradations of a color can give movement to a design.

Let's Play with Color and Value

1   Start EQ5.

2   Choose Create a New Project.

3   Type the name for your new project: C Value - Floating Fans.

4   Click OK.

5   Click Worktable — Work on Quilt.

Steps 2-4

Design the Quilt

Layout

6   Click Quilt — New Quilt — On-point.

7   Click the Layout tab along the bottom of the screen.

8   Under Number of blocks, click the arrows to read 2 Horizontal and 2 Vertical.

9   Under Size of blocks, drag the slider to read 10.00.

10 Under Sashing, drag the slider to read 1.75.

Border

11 Click the Borders tab along the bottom of the screen.

12 Be sure there is a check next to All under Adjust Size. (Clicking will turn this check on and off.)

13 Drag one of the sliders to read 3.00. All sides will adjust automatically.

14 Click the Layer 1 tab along the bottom of the screen.

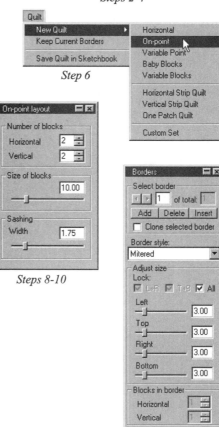

Step 6

Steps 8-10

Steps 12-13

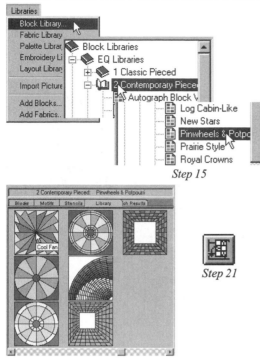

Step 15

Steps 17-18

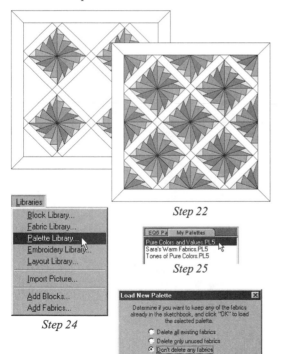

Step 22

Step 24

Step 25

Step 27

Step 21

Block

15 Click Libraries — Block Library — EQ Libraries — 2 Contemporary Pieced — Pinwheels & Potpourri.

16 Drag the horizontal scrollbar below the blocks to the right to see all the blocks in this book.

17 We want the Cool Fan block. Position your cursor over a block and the block name will appear.

18 Click on the Cool Fan block to select it. You'll see a frame around it to know it's the selected one.

19 Click Copy. You'll notice that the block temporarily disappears, indicating you've "copied" it into your Sketchbook.

20 Click Close.

21 Click the Set tool.

22 Position your cursor over any block space in your empty quilt layout. (This is an On-point quilt layout, so you need to think in two's.)

Hold down your keyboard CTRL key and click. One "row" of your on-point quilt will fill. While still holding down the CTRL key, click another empty block space. Your quilt is now filled with Cool Fan blocks.

Collect the Colors for the Quilt

23 Click Libraries — Palette Library.

24 Click on the My Palettes tab behind the EQ5 Palettes tab.

25 Click on the Pure Colors and Values palette.

26 Click the Load button. A message will pop up, asking what to do with the current fabric palette.

27 Click "Don't delete any fabrics," then OK.

3

Color the Floating Fans Quilt

See how the fans are already colored in a gradation of cool colors. Let's build on this.

28 Before you begin to change the quilt, click the Save in Sketchbook button.

Step 28

29 Click the Swap tool.

Step 29

30 Click the Solids tab on the palette.

31 Find and click on **black**.

32 Click the border with the Swap tool, then click the tiny triangles outside the fan. This will swap white or cream wherever it appears in your quilt. It puts black into:

- The border
- The sashing and sash squares
- The tiny, background triangles next to each point of the fan.

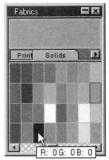
Step 31

Step 32

33 Click the Paintbrush tool.

You will color each block with 8 graded values from dark to light. Notice that the block is divided into 2 sides, and that each side contains 8 pieces. Color both sides the same, always beginning at the top of the right side and the bottom of the left side. **Notice that to color all blocks, you will have to** *do the CTRL + click process twice for Steps 35-37*, **because there are two sets of blocks.**

Step 33

34 Scroll through the Solids palette and find the Shades and Tints of **pure yellow-green**. Use only the middle eight values.

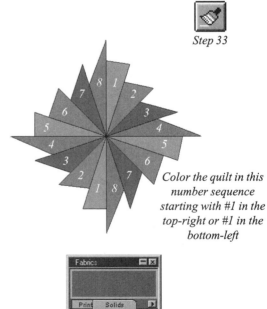
Color the quilt in this number sequence starting with #1 in the top-right or #1 in the bottom-left

✎ Tip

If you can't distinguish your green values from those for yellow-green, use any of the following to find the set:

• Click the third lightest value of each set, and use the set that looks like it has more yellow in it

• The RGB tooltips for yellow-green will have higher numbers for R than green.

• Find pure yellow-green at the beginning of the palette and right-click to add Shades and Tints again.

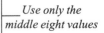
Use only the middle eight values

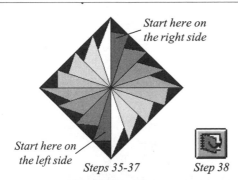

Start here on the right side

Start here on the left side

Steps 35-37

Step 38

Yellow-green quilt

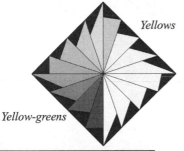

Yellows

Yellow-greens

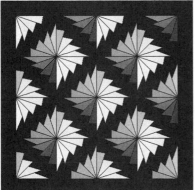

Steps 40-42

Step 43

35 Click on the **second darkest value of yellow-green** and CTRL + click to place it in the top-right patch of every block, and then diagonally opposite of it in the bottom-left patch of each block.

36 Click on the **third darkest value** and place it into the second fan patches.

37 Continue around the block, working through the eight values.

38 Click the Save in Sketchbook button.

Look at the quilt. Notice how the bright yellow-green glows on the black background. Let's see what happens when we add the values of a second color.

Add Yellow to the Next Quilt

39 Scroll through the Solids Palette, find the Shades and Tints of **pure yellow**. Use the middle eight values.

You will add yellow to the *right sides only* of each block so that when the quilt is finished it will contain two-color gradations, yellow-green on the left and yellow on the right.

40 Click on the **second darkest value of yellow** and CTRL + click to place it in the top-right patch of every block.

41 Click on the **third darkest value** and place it into the second fan patch.

42 Continue around the right side of the block, working through the eight values.

43 Click the Save in Sketchbook button.

Notice how the addition of a second color adds interest to the quilt.

3

Add Blue-Green to the Next Quilt

Now that your blocks are colored in halves, you can swap out the colors on one side for a new set of colors without having to do it twice.

44 Click the Swap tool.

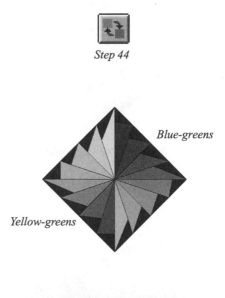

Step 44

45 Scroll through the Solids Palette, find the Shades and Tints of **pure blue-green**. Use the middle eight values.

You will replace the yellow with the blue green on the right sides of all the blocks. When the quilt is finished it will contain two color gradations, yellow-green on the left and blue-green on the right.

46 Click on the **second darkest value of blue-green** and click to place it in the top-right patch of every block.

47 Click on the **third darkest value** and place it into the second fan patch.

48 Continue around the right side of the block, working through the eight values.

49 Click the Save in Sketchbook button. Notice how the quilt changes when switched to a cool color.

Blue-greens

Yellow-greens

Add Blue to the Blocks

You will replace the yellow-green with the blue on the *left sides* of all the blocks. When the quilt is finished it will contain color gradations of two analogous colors, blue on the left and blue-green on the right.

50 Scroll through the Solids Palette, find the Shades and Tints of **pure blue**. Use the middle eight values.

51 Click on the **second darkest value of blue** and CTRL + click to place it in the bottom-left patch of every block.

Steps 46-48

Step 49

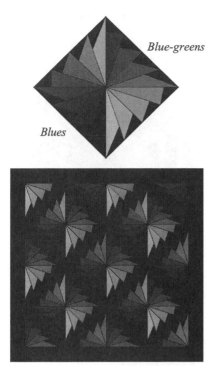

Blue-greens

Blues

Steps 51-53

Step 54

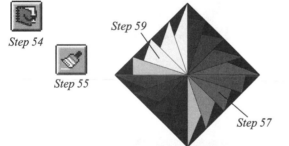

Step 55

Step 59

Step 57

Fan Variation

52 Click on the **third darkest value** and place it into the second fan patch.

53 Continue around the left side of the block, working through the eight values.

54 Click the Save in Sketchbook button. Notice how the quilt changes now with analogous colors.

Try More Variations

You have been varying the two sides of the quilt design. Notice that the block actually contains four identical quadrants. You can add more interest to the block by adding a third and fourth color, so that every quadrant is different. If you use analogous colors, the fans will appear to spin like the pinwheels they are.

55 Click the Paintbrush tool.

56 Find the Shades and Tints of **red-violet**.

57 Use four of the middle values. CTRL + click in the bottom-right quadrant to replace the lightest blue-greens.

3

58 Find the Shades and Tints of **yellow**.

59 Use four of the middle values. CTRL + click in the top-left quadrant to replace the lightest blues.

60 Click the Save in Sketchbook button.

Try some more variations of your own, following steps 55-60 to add many values of any colors you like. Click the Save in Sketchbook button for each quilt.

If you want, you can try:

- Analogous fans with red, red-orange, orange, and yellow-orange.

- A cool fan quilt with four analogous colors.

- Complementary fans with the values of only the two colors.

Study your Floating Fans &
Remember What You Learned

- Click the View Sketchbook button and then the Quilts tab. Use the arrows to flip through a slide show of the different versions of your Floating Fans quilt.

- Notice what parts of the block stand out.

- Notice how value gradations of a color give movement to a design.

- Remember this trick in EQ5: I wanted to design a quilt with more space between blocks, so I added sashing and colored it in the same color as the block background. This would work in real life quiltmaking, too.

Study your Floating Fans

3

Practice with Value and Saturation

Let's Play with Color, Saturation and Tones

1   Start EQ5.

2   Choose Create a New Project.

3   Type the name for your new project:
C Value - Cross Patch.

4   Click OK.

Collect the Colors for Quilt 1

5   Click Libraries — Palette Library.

6   Click on the My Palettes tab behind the EQ Palettes tab.

7   Click on the Pure Colors and Values palette.

8   Click the Load button. A message will pop up, asking what to do with the current fabric palette.

9   Click "Delete all existing fabrics," then OK.

Design the Five-Patch Block

10   Click Worktable — Work on Block.

11   Click Block — New Block — EasyDraw™.

12   Click Block — Drawing Board Setup. You will be on the General tab.

13   Under Snap to Grid Points, the first number will be blue to show it is selected. Type in 25 for the Horizontal divisions.

14   Press the TAB key on your keyboard and type 25 for the Vertical divisions.

15   Press TAB and type 5 for the Horizontal block size, then press TAB and type 5 for the Vertical block size.

16   Click over to the Graph Paper tab.

17   Under Options, click the dropdown arrow for Style and set it to Blank, then click OK.

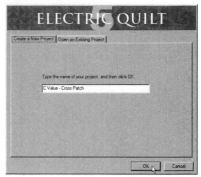

Steps 2-4

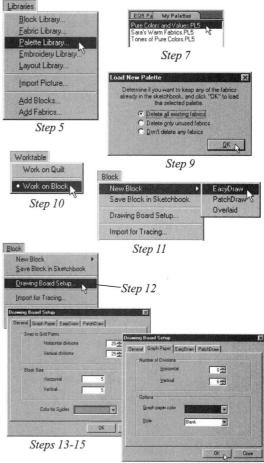

Step 7

Step 9

Step 10

Step 11

Step 12

Steps 13-15

Step 17 — The number of graph paper divisions does not matter because we are setting them not to show (Blank)

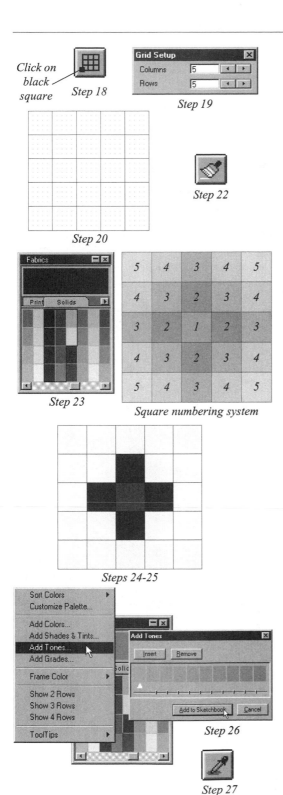

Click on black square *Step 18*

Step 19

Step 20

Step 22

Fabrics

Step 23

5	4	3	4	5
4	3	2	3	4
3	2	1	2	3
4	3	2	3	4
5	4	3	4	5

Square numbering system

Steps 24-25

Sort Colors
Customize Palette...

Add Colors...
Add Shades & Tints...
Add Tones...
Add Grades...

Frame Color

Show 2 Rows
Show 3 Rows
Show 4 Rows

ToolTips

Add Tones

Insert   Remove

Add to Sketchbook   Cancel

Step 26

Step 27

18 Click the Grid tool. To access the Grid tool setup, click on the tiny black square in the lower-left corner of the button or right-click on the Block Worktable and choose Grid setup.

19 Set the Grid setup to 5 columns by 5 rows.

20 Click on any corner of the block outline and drag your cursor to the opposite corner of the block outline. The five-patch layout will appear. Release your cursor when done.

Color a Blue Saturation Block

21 Click the Color tab along the bottom of your screen.

22 Click the Paintbrush tool, then the Solids tab. You are going to make five versions of the five-patch in five different colors.

23 Scroll to find the Shades and Tints of **pure blue**.

24 Click on the **fifth darkest value**, then click in the center square of your block.

25 Click on the **second darkest blue** and click it into the four #2 squares next to the center square to form a cross.

26 Right-click on the **third lightest value** and choose Add Tones. Click Add to Sketchbook.

27 Click the Eyedropper tool and click in the center square to pick up your blue. You will be moved in the palette to the Shades and Tints of blue.

3

28 Right-click on the **next lightest value** (from the one you're on) and choose Add Tones. Click Add to Sketchbook.

29 Scroll to see the two sets of tones at the far right end of the palette.

In the next steps, be sure to work with these dull tones (the last two sets on the far right), and not the shades and tints.

30 Click on a **medium blue tone** that still has some color. Put it into the eight #3 squares.

31 Click on a **lighter blue tone** and put it into the eight #4 squares.

32 Click on the **lightest blue tone** (it will look plain gray, but it actually has a blue cast). Put this into the #5 squares.

33 Click the Save in Sketchbook button.

Sit back and look at your little plaid block. It does two things:

- Shows how the grayed tones come from a pure color.

- Contrasts low-saturation tones with their high-saturation pure color.

Color a Red-violet Saturation Block

34 Return to the Solids palette and find the Shades and Tints of **pure red-violet**.

35 Repeat Steps 23-33 using tones of red-violet instead of blue.

36 Follow Steps 23-33, and color a:

- **Red** Saturation Block

- **Violet** Saturation Block

- **Blue-green** Saturation Block

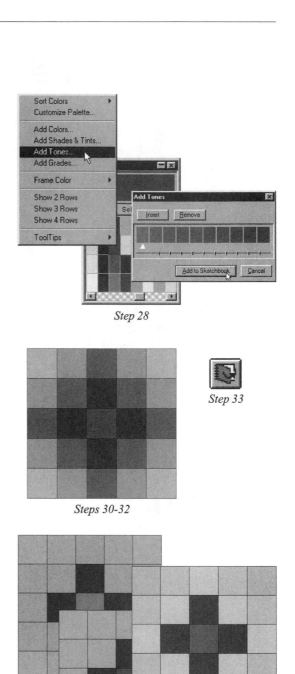

Step 28

Step 33

Steps 30-32

Red

Blue-green

Violet

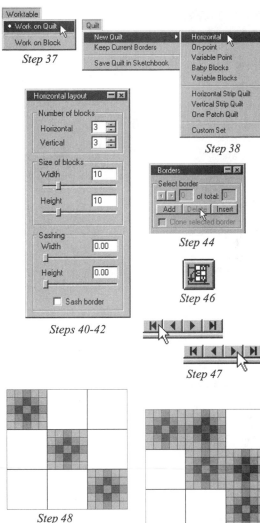

Step 37

Step 38

Steps 40-42

Step 44

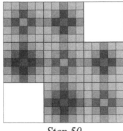

Step 46

Step 47

Step 48

Step 49

Step 50

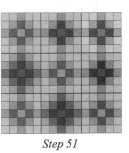

Step 51

Step 52

Design the Quilt

Layout

37 Click Worktable — Work on Quilt.

38 Click Quilt — New Quilt — Horizontal.

39 Click the Layout tab along the bottom of the screen.

40 Under Number of blocks, click the arrows to read 3 Horizontal and 3 Vertical.

41 Under Size of blocks, drag the sliders to read 10.00 Width and 10.00 Height.

42 Under Sashing, drag both the sliders to read 0.00.

Border

43 Click the Borders tab along the bottom of the screen.

44 Click the Delete button to eliminate any borders.

45 Click the Layer 1 tab.

Set the Blocks

46 Click the Set tool, then the Blocks tab.

47 Click your block to select it. Click the first colorway arrow to go to the line drawing of your block. Use the third colorway arrow to scroll through the colorings made earlier.

48 Choose your favorite coloring and click it into a diagonal row going from top-left to bottom-right on your quilt.

49 Use the colorway arrows to select a different coloration, and put it in the diagonal row above the center row.

50 Put a different coloration in the diagonal row below the center row.

51 In the bottom-left and top-right corners, put the fourth and fifth colorations.

52 Save the quilt in the Sketchbook.

3

Study your quilt. It is simple gradations of saturation that provide some contrast.

Quilt 2

53 Click the Borders tab.

54 Click Add to make one border. Leave this border so all sides are 1.00 and the style is set to Mitered.

55 Click the Layer 1 tab.

56 Color the border in a **very grayed color** of your choice. Try several, saving each quilt in the Sketchbook.

Notice that this is still a simple quilt. The binding is a way to pick up a color you like and to add a finished look to the quilt.

Quilt 3

57 Click the Borders tab.

58 Under Border style, change to Corner Blocks.

59 Be sure there is a check next to All under Adjust Size. (Clicking will turn this check on and off.)

60 Make the width 2.00. All sides will adjust automatically.

61 Click the Layer 1 tab.

62 Use a **medium tone** of a color in the border.

63 In the corner squares, use **medium tones** of four different colors.

64 Save Quilt 3 in the Sketchbook.

Look how this border echoes the block design, bringing the design out into the border. This is a good way to tie the center and border together.

Step 54

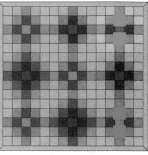

Step 56

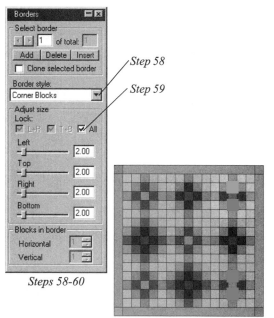

Step 58

Step 59

Steps 58-60

Steps 62-63

Step 64

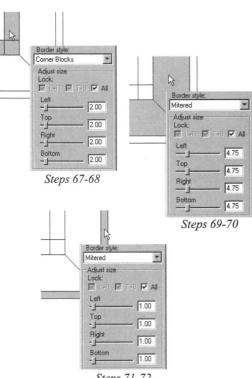

Steps 67-68

Steps 69-70

Steps 71-72

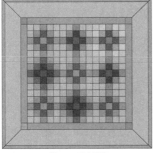

Steps 74-76

Step 77

Step 79

Quilt 4

65 Click the Borders tab.

66 Click the Add button twice to make a total of 3 borders.

67 Click on the inner border.

68 Make sure all sides are 2.00 and the style is set to Corner Blocks.

69 Click on the middle border.

70 Under Border Style, choose Mitered. Make the width 4.75. All sides will adjust automatically.

71 Click on the outer border.

72 Under Border Style, choose Mitered. Make the width 1.00.

73 Click the Layer 1 tab.

74 Color the middle border first. Use **an almost pure gray** in any color you like (when in doubt, choose a cool color).

75 Color the inner and outer borders **a medium tone of any color**.

76 In the corner squares of the inner border, use **medium tones** of four different colors.

77 Save Quilt 4 in the Sketchbook.

Look how the corner squares of the inner border tie the quilt together. The squares are the same size as those of the five patches (2.00), enhancing the effect.

Quilt 5

78 Click the Layout tab.

79 Under Sashing, drag the sliders to read 2.00. Be sure Sash border is *not* checked. (Clicking here will turn this check on and off.)

80 Click the Layer 1 tab.

3

81 Color the sashing and cross squares in the same colors as the inner border. Keep the coloration from Quilt 4 or change the borders.

82 Save this quilt in the Sketchbook.

Study the quilt. Notice how adding the sashing alters the design. It divides the gradation but echoes the pattern. It is not better — just a different and equally effective treatment.

Quilt 6
83 Click the Borders tab.

84 Click on the middle border.

85 Change the Border style to Corner Blocks.

86 Change the border size to 8.00.

87 Click the Layer 1 tab.

88 Click the Set tool.

89 Click to place a different colored five-patch block into each of the four corners.

90 Color or recolor any or all of the borders to make a pretty quilt. Continue to use the tones.

91 Save Quilt 6 in the Sketchbook.

Quilt 7
92 Click Quilt — New Quilt — On-point.

93 Click the Layout tab.

94 Under Number of blocks, click the arrows to read 3 Horizontal and 3 Vertical.

95 Under Size of blocks, drag the slider to read 8.00.

96 Under Sashing, drag the slider to 0.00 to eliminate all sashing.

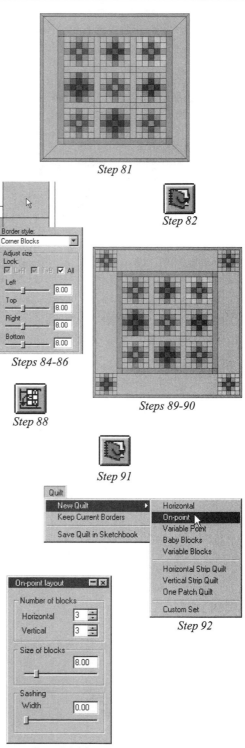

Step 81

Step 82

Steps 84-86

Step 88

Steps 89-90

Step 91

Step 92

Steps 94-96

Step 100

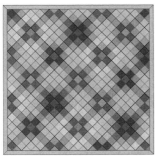

Step 101

Step 102

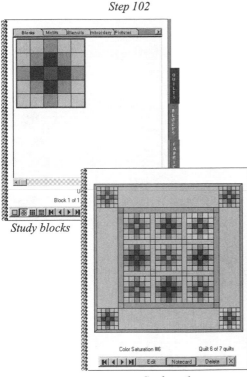

Study blocks

Study quilts

97 Click the Borders tab.

98 If you do not already have a 1.00 mitered border on your quilt, create one.

99 Click the Layer 1 tab.

100 Click the Set tool.

101 Place different colored blocks into the quilt at random or in an organized way. Fill the blocks around the edge, too. Use all of your colorations. Color the border to match the quilt.

102 Save Quilt 7 in the Sketchbook.

Study your Saturation Quilts & Remember What You Learned

• Click the View Sketchbook button, then the Quilts tab. Use the arrows to flip through a slide show of the different versions of the Saturation blocks.

• Notice how the pure center surrounded by its dark value stands out. Pure colors are always stronger than their tones, and dark is always strong, too.

• The different borders and the addition of sashing change the design.

• Notice how gradations of tones give movement to a design.

• Playing with saturation in a quilt is one of the Tried and True formulas in color theory. Think of plaids — varied saturation is exactly what creates a plaid.

3

Contrast in Temperature of Warm and Cool Colors

Color Theory

This fun and simple lesson focuses on warm and cool colors. We will experiment with their placement in a simple star on a plain background. Enjoy!

Let's Play with the Bright Star

1 Start EQ5.

2 Choose Create a New Project.

3 Type the name for your new project: C Warm-Cool Contrast - Bright Star.

4 Click OK.

5 Click Worktable — Work on Quilt.

Design the Quilt

Layout

6 Click Quilt — New Quilt — Horizontal.

7 Click the Layout tab along the bottom of the screen.

8 Under Number of blocks, click the arrows to read 1 Horizontal and 1 Vertical.

9 Under Size of blocks, drag the sliders to read 20.00 Width and 20.00 Height.

10 Since there is only one block, don't worry about the numbers for sashing. Let's work on the borders now.

Borders

11 Click the Borders tab along the bottom of the screen.

12 Click the Add button once to make a total of two borders.

13 Be sure there is a check next to All under Adjust size. (Clicking will turn this check on and off.)

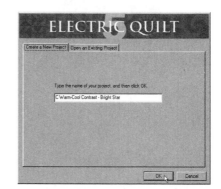

Steps 2-4

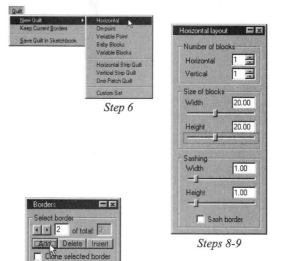

Step 6

Steps 8-9

Step 12

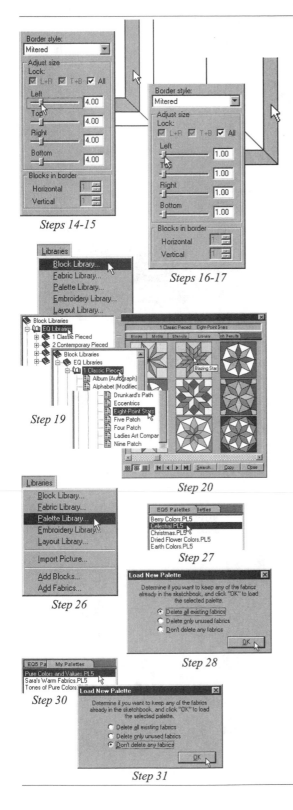

Steps 14-15

Steps 16-17

Step 19

Step 20

Step 26

Step 27

Step 28

Step 30

Step 31

14 Click on the inner border.

15 Drag one of the sliders to 4.00.

16 Click on the outer border.

17 Drag one of the sliders to 1.00.

18 Click the Layer 1 tab along the bottom of the screen.

Block

19 Click Libraries — Block Library — EQ Libraries — 1 Classic Pieced — Eight-Point Stars. The blocks in this book will appear.

20 Find and click on the Blazing Star block. If your view is still set to nine blocks at a time, it is the second block in the top row.

21 Click Copy. You'll notice that the block temporarily disappears, indicating you've "copied" it into your Sketchbook.

22 Click Close.

23 Click the Set tool, and then the Blocks tab.

24 Click on the Blazing Star block to select it.

25 Click in the center of your quilt. The Blazing Star block will appear.

Collect the Fabrics for the Quilt

26 Click Libraries — Palette Library — EQ5 Palettes tab.

27 Click the Celestial palette to select it and click Load.

28 Choose "Delete all existing fabrics," then click OK.

29 Click Libaries — Palette Library — My Palettes tab.

30 Click your Pure Colors and Values palette to select it and click Load.

31 Choose "Don't delete any fabrics," and click OK.

3

32 Click the Paintbrush tool.

Step 32

33 Click the Prints tab and scroll through the fabrics to remind yourself of the fabrics available.

Quilt 1: Warm on Cool

34 Find and click on a **dark orange** print in the palette.

35 Click on the eight diamonds in the center of the star.

36 Find and click on a **medium orange** print.

37 Click on the diamonds surrounding the center eight. CTRL + click on the outer border.

Step 35

38 Find and click on a **pure yellow** print.

39 Click on the eight diamonds at the endpoints of the star.

Step 37

40 Find and click on a **dark blue** print.

41 Click the Spraycan tool (not the EQ4 Spraycan). Click in the background of your Blazing Star block.

42 CTRL + click on the inner border.

43 Click the Save in Sketchbook button. You now have a yellow star on dark blue background.

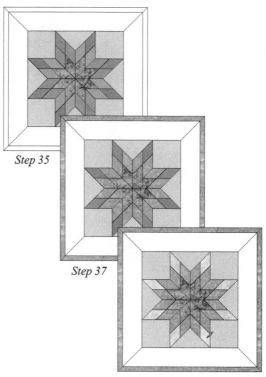

Step 39

Color Other Quilts

44 Follow these guidelines in each quilt:

Step 41   *Step 43*

- Work with prints and in bright, pure colors.

- In the star, use a variety of values of one color, with the brightest on the outer points.

- Treat the background and inner border as one unit and use one fabric.

Final Bright Star Quilt

3

Quilt 3

Quilt 4

Quilt 5

Quilt 6

Save in Sketchbook

View your quilts in the Sketchbook

- Use the outer border to repeat a color from the star.

- Make one quilt in each of these styles:

Quilt 2: Same yellow star on a different dark blue background.

Quilt 3: Blue star on a yellow background.

Quilt 4: Red and orange star on a dark blue background.

Quilt 5: An all red star on a pure blue background.

Quilt 6: Pure blue star on a pure red background.

- Save each quilt in your Sketchbook.

Study Your Quilts and Remember

- Click the View Sketchbook button and then the Quilts tab. Use the arrows to scroll through the quilts from first to last.

- Look at what colors catch your eye first.

- Which quilts are successful? Which are unsuccessful? See if you can notice a trend in your color placement that makes some stars stand out or others fade into the background.

- Cool and warm colors behave differently when put together. In the next chapter, we'll learn the how and why of this behavior.

3

More Warm and Cool Contrast

Let's Play with Warm-Cool Contrast

1 Start EQ5.

2 Choose Create a New Project.

3 Type the name for your new project:
C Warm-Cool Contrast - Kansas Beauty.

4 Click OK.

5 Click Worktable — Work on Quilt.

Design the Quilt

Layout

6 Click Quilt — New Quilt — Horizontal.

7 Click the Layout tab along the bottom of the screen.

8 Under Number of blocks, click the arrows to read 2 Horizontal and 2 Vertical.

9 Under Size of blocks, drag the sliders to read 12.00 Width and 12.00 Height.

10 Under Sashing, drag both the sliders to read 0.00 to eliminate the sashing.

Borders

11 Click the Borders tab along the bottom of the screen.

12 You should have one border, click the Add button if you do not have one border already.

13 Be sure there is a check next to All under Adjust size. (Clicking will turn this check on and off.)

14 Drag one of the sliders to 4.50. All sides will adjust automatically.

15 Click the Layer 1 tab along the bottom of the screen.

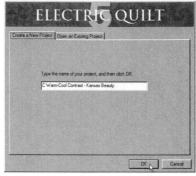

Step 2-4

Step 6

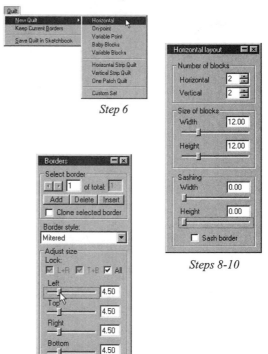

Steps 8-10

Step 14

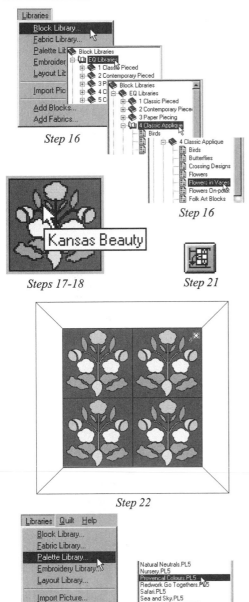

Step 16

Step 16

Steps 17-18

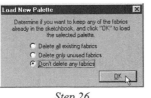

Step 21

Step 22

Step 23

Step 24

Step 26

Block

16 Click Libraries — Block Library — EQ Libraries — 4 Classic Appliqué — Flowers in Vases. The blocks in this book will appear.

17 Drag the horizontal scrollbar below the blocks to the right to see everything in this book. We want the Kansas Beauty block, which is the second-to-last block in this category. If you position your cursor over a block, the block name appears to help you find the block you want.

18 Click on the Kansas Beauty block to select it.

19 Click Copy. You'll notice that the block temporarily disappears, indicating you've "copied" it into your Sketchbook.

20 Click Close.

21 Click the Set tool, then the Blocks tab. Click on the block to select it.

22 Position your cursor over any block space in your empty quilt layout. Hold down your keyboard CTRL key and click. Your quilt is now filled with Kansas Beauty blocks.

Collect the Fabrics for the Quilt

For this quilt, you will use the basic palette plus some other fabrics. We're going to collect some of the computer-generated fabrics to show how you can also use these in your quilt. Be sure to get a good mix of warm, cool, shades, tints, and tones of the primary colors.

23 Click Libraries — Palette Library — EQ5 Palettes tab.

24 Click on the Provencal Colours palette.

25 Click Load.

26 Choose "Don't delete any fabrics," and click OK.

3

27 Click Libraries — Fabric Library — EQ Libraries.

28 Click on Designer Fabric Basics — P& B Textiles.

29 Copy at least 10 fabrics that are pure primary colors, their shades, tints, or tones. Stay away from neutrals and other non-colors.

30 Scroll down in the Fabric Library list and click on EQ3 Packet Fabrics.

31 Collect 10 fabrics from each of these packets:

- 1950s Apron Packet
- '40s Sherbet Prints
- Blue and White

32 Click Close.

Color the Quilt

You are now ready to color several versions of the Kansas Beauty quilt. On all colorings, use CTRL + click to fill all pieces of the appliqué design in all blocks at the same time. Keep all four blocks colored the same way.

33 Click the Paintbrush tool.

34 Click on the Prints tab in the palette. Scroll through the swatches to see the fabrics now available. The added fabrics are at the right end.

Cool Kansas Beauty Quilt 1

In this quilt, be sure to work entirely in the cool colors from the left side of the color wheel. Use several fabrics in a variety of values and textures to create a pretty quilt. Avoid cool fabrics that contain strong warm colors.

35 Find a **light blue** in the palette. CTRL + click to color the block background.

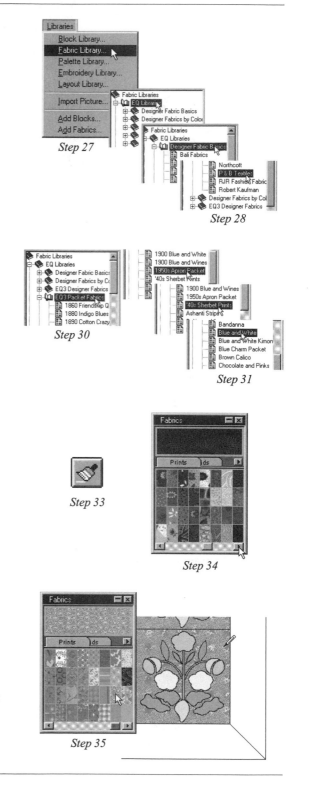

Step 27

Step 28

Step 30

Step 31

Step 33

Step 34

Step 35

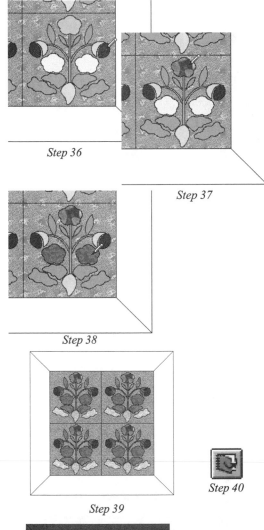

Step 36

Step 37

Step 38

Step 39

Step 40

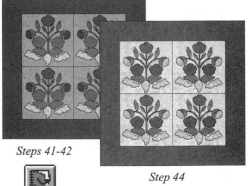

Steps 41-42

Step 44

Step 45

36 Find a **dark blue**. CTRL + click the border. CTRL + click the two pale orange buds in the block.

37 Find a **different dark blue**. CTRL + click the top flower in the block.

38 Find a **medium violet**. CTRL + click the two pale yellow flowers in the middle of the block.

39 The rest of the block will be green. Use a **dark green** on the stems, a **light green** on the two motifs at the bottom of the block, and **various medium greens** everywhere that is still uncolored.

40 Save this quilt in the Sketchbook.

Cool Kansas Beauty Quilt 2

41 Make another cool quilt, but change the quantities, colors and prints. Don't forget the flashy pastels you got from the library. Try them, too.

42 Try different fabrics in the border until you find one you like.

43 Save Quilt 2 in the Sketchbook.

Warm Kansas Beauty Quilts 3 and 4

44 Repeat Steps 35-39, but use only warm colors to create two different warm quilts. Try using red for the flowers and yellow or orange for the buds. You may use green for the leaves if you want. Avoid warm fabrics that contain strong cool colors.

45 Save both warm quilts in your Sketchbook.

3

Warm and Cool Kansas Beauty
Quilts 5 and 6

46 Make two more quilts, but this time use a combination of warm and cool colors. Try using blue in the flowers, and red in the buds as well as the border.

47 Save this quilt in the Sketchbook.

48 Try other warm-cool quilts. Save them in the Sketchbook. Use any warm or cool colors you like. Just keep the block background light and the border a fabric repeated from the quilt center. This gives you total freedom and should make for very lively quilts.

Study Your Warm and Cool Quilts

• Click the View Sketchbook button, then the Quilts tab. Use the arrows to flip through a slide show of the different versions of your Kansas Beauty quilts. Go from the first quilt through the last.

• Are the cool-only quilts quieter?

• Are the warm-only quilts livelier?

• When you combine warm and cool colors, are the quilts stronger?

• Which quilts do you like best or least? Why?

Remember

• Warm and cool colors are different and create different moods.

• Cool colors soothe, while warm colors stimulate.

• Warm and cool colors together make a strong, vibrant contrast.

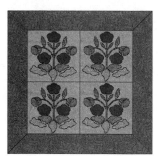

Step 47

Step 46

View your Sketchbook

Warm - Cool Mix   Quilt 6 of 6 quilts

View your quilts in your Sketchbook

CHAPTER 3
Complementary and Analogous Colors

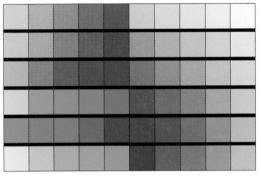

Complementary colors in several values

Two complements create a striking Setting Sun quilt

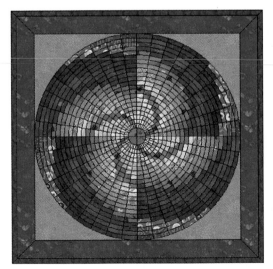

Analogous colors from red through yellow make this swirling analogous quilt spin

Analogous colors from violet through green create a cool Swirls quilt

PAGES 58 & 70

CHAPTER 3
Value and Saturation

*Value gradation in blue and yellow-green
creates movement in Floating Fans*

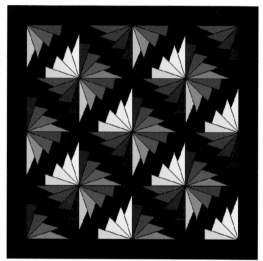

*Value gradation in warm and cool colors
creates movement in Floating Fans*

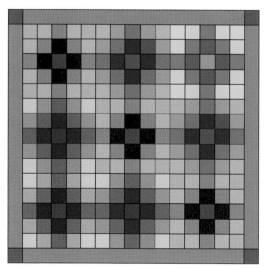

*Gradation of tones creates soft contrast and
gentle movement*

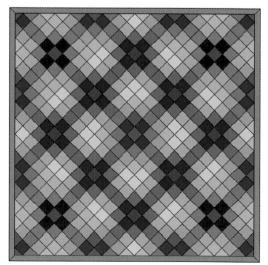

*Gradation of tones in analogous colors
brings movement to a simple design*

PAGES 76 & 84

A warm star sparkles on a cool background

A cool star fades into a hot background

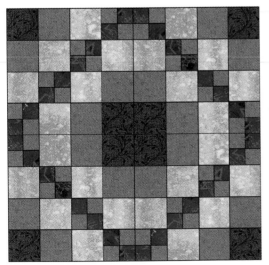

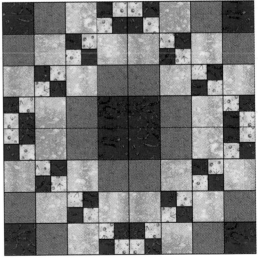

A warm red diamond advances on a cool blue background

Warm, pure red and yellow dictate the diamond design

PAGES 92 & 106

CHAPTER 4
How Colors Behave

Color temperature is relative; red-violet is the warmest color in this Broken Sash quilt

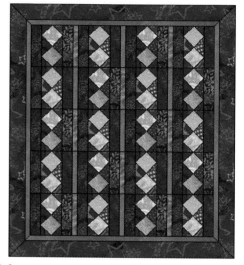

Color temperature is relative; red-violet is the coolest color in this Broken Sash quilt

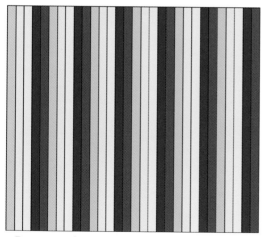

Pure complements placed together intensify each other and create strong simultaneous contrast

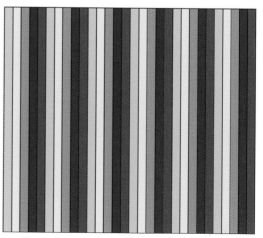

Gray can soften and dilute simultaneous contrast

PAGES 114 & 122

How Colors Behave

Chapter 4

Warm Advances and Cool Recedes

Color Theory

Colors behave differently when placed together. Some are strong and want to take over; they come forward or advance, no matter where you put them in your quilt design. Others like to recede and become background no matter where they are placed. If we can understand which colors dominate others, we can take control of our quilt designs.

Warm colors are stronger than cool colors. Even if you put them in what you consider the background, they will take over. Cool colors, on the other hand, recede and become background, even when placed in the focal point of a quilt.

The pure colors of the color wheel are stronger than tones. Pure will always advance when combined with low intensity, grayed colors.

Although colors have strength, the *quantity of a color in a quilt also affects its strength.* Use a lot of one color and it will stand out just because of its proportion to the other colors of the quilt.

Strong colors will advance even if they are used only in small quantities.

Dark and light values are less predictable, but they tend to be strong enough to define your design. The dominance is likely to depend on the quantity of color used; light colors will advance on a mostly-dark quilt, as will dark colors on a mostly-light quilt.

Let's See if We Can Control the Warm-Cool Design

1   Start EQ5.

2   Choose Create a New Project.

3   Type the name for your new project: C Advance and Recede – Carrie Nation.

4   Click OK.

The cool light blue block recedes behind the pure red to become background

The warm pure red block advances over the light blue block

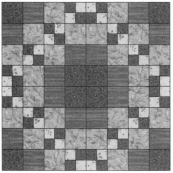

Notice how the warm-colored diamond shape stands out against the cool background.

Steps 2-4

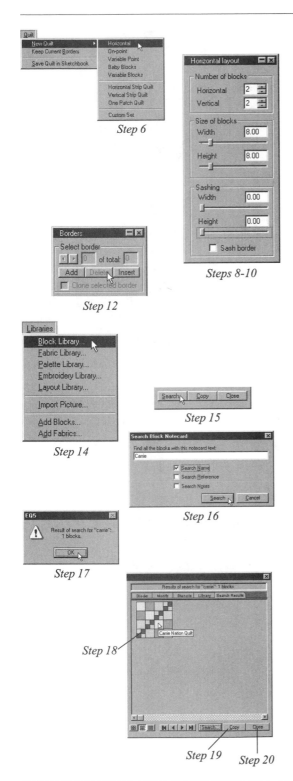

Step 6

Steps 8-10

Step 12

Step 14

Step 15

Step 16

Step 17

Step 18

Step 19   *Step 20*

5   Click Worktable — Work on Quilt.

Design the Quilt

Layout

6   Click Quilt — New Quilt — Horizontal.

7   Click the Layout tab along the bottom of the screen.

8   Under Number of blocks, click the arrows to read 2 Horizontal and 2 Vertical.

9   Under Size of blocks, drag the sliders to read 8.00 Width and 8.00 Height.

10 Under Sashing, drag both the sliders to read 0.00 to eliminate the sashing.

Borders

11 Click the Borders tab along the bottom of the screen.

12 Click the Delete button so you have no border.

13 Click the Layer 1 tab along the bottom of the screen.

Block

14 Click Libraries — Block Library.

15 Click the Search button.

16 You want the Carrie Nation Quilt block, so type in the word "Carrie" and click Search.

17 Click OK when the results are returned.

18 Click on the Carrie Nation Quilt block to select it.

19 Click Copy. You'll notice that the block temporarily disappears, indicating you've "copied" it into your Sketchbook.

20 Click Close.

4

21 Click the Set tool, then the Blocks tab. Click the Carrie Nation Quilt block to select it.

Look at the block. Notice that it contains 16 squares, 8 of which are subdivided into tiny 4 patches. Notice also how the tiny purple squares seem to march across the block, standing out because of color: the dark pure purple stands out against the pale cool colors of the other squares.

22 Position your cursor over any block space in your empty quilt layout. CTRL + click to fill your quilt with the block.

23 Click the Rotate tool.

24 Rotate two of the blocks so the design is a diamond. (Rotate the top-right block and the bottom-left block once each.)

Collect the Fabrics

We are only going to use the primary colors and some of their values for this lesson, so let's clear the other fabrics in your Sketchbook.

25 Click the View Sketchbook button, then click the Fabrics tab.

26 Click Clear.

27 Click OK on the Clear Fabric Sketchbook box. Your fabrics will disappear.

28 Click the X to close the Sketchbook.

29 Click Libraries — Fabric Library — EQ Libraries — Designer Fabrics by Color.

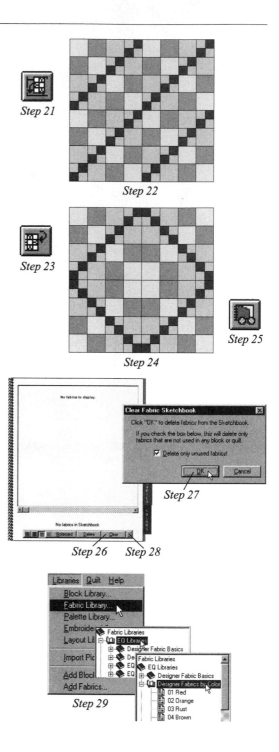

Step 21

Step 22

Step 23

Step 24

Step 25

Step 27

Step 26   *Step 28*

Step 29

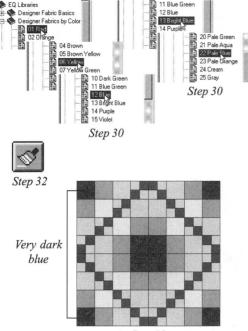

Step 30

Step 30

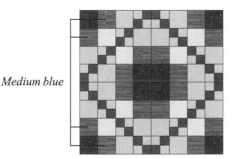

Step 32

Very dark
blue

Step 33

Medium blue

Steps 34-35

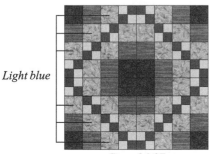

Light blue

Steps 36-37

30 Copy 6-8 fabrics from each of these books:

01 Red

06 Yellow

12 Blue

13 Bright Blue

22 Pale Blue

31 Click Close. You are back on the quilt worktable.

Color the Quilt Blue

We're going to color this quilt like a Trip Around the World quilt — diamond bands of color progressing outward — in a monochromatic color scheme at first. We will need four values of blue for this monochromatic quilt. To help you know where to color, I will refer to the large squares and the mini-4-patch squares.

32 Click the Paintbrush tool. Click the Prints tab on the palette.

33 Choose a **very dark blue**. CTRL + click to color the top-left and bottom-left corners. This should color each large corner square and the four large squares in the center.

34 Choose a **medium blue**. Look at the top-left corner of the quilt; we're going to replace the two darker teal squares. CTRL + click to color once below and one more time to the right of the corner.

35 Look at the bottom-left corner of the quilt. CTRL + click to color the large squares above and to the right of the corner.

36 Choose a **light blue**. Look at the top-left corner of your quilt. CTRL + click the three squares on the diagonal next to your medium blue.

37 Look at the bottom-left corner of your quilt. CTRL + click the three squares on the diagonal next to your medium blue.

4

38 Click the Swap tool.

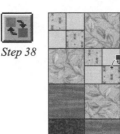

Step 38

39 Choose **very pale blue**. Click to replace the dark purple mini-4-patch squares.

40 Click the Eyedropper tool.

41 Click in your quilt on the medium blue you used earlier in Steps 34-35. The Eyedropper will pick up that color and switch you over to the Swap tool.

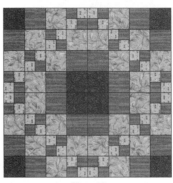

Step 40

Step 39

42 Click to replace the light purple mini-4-patch squares.

43 Click Save in Sketchbook.

Add Red to Your Quilt

Look at your quilt for a while, and notice how it all seems pretty evenly colored.

44 Find any **pure red** in the palette. Click with the Swap tool to replace the very pale blue in the quilt.

Step 43

45 Click Save in Sketchbook.

46 Find your pale blue in the palette and click to replace the red. Watch how your quilt design changes.

Step 42

47 Swap between red and pale blue once or twice and watch the quilt design.

4

Look at your quilt as you do this and see how the quilt changes when red is added. Red stands out because it is warm and pure. With the diamond colored red it becomes the first thing you see. Using red in this manner enhances the overall diamond design of the quilt. (Proceed to the next step when your quilt is blue only.)

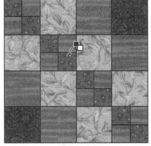

Step 45

Step 44

48 Now, using this same red, click to replace the dark blue center. The four center squares and four corner squares will now be red.

49 Click Save in Sketchbook.

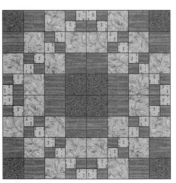

Step 49

Step 48

Step 51

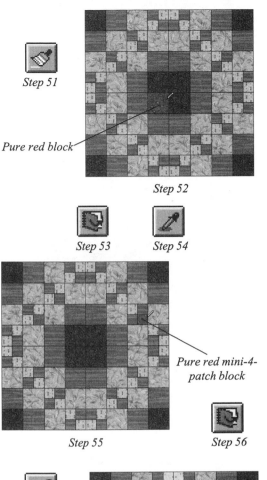

Pure red block

Step 52

Step 53

Step 54

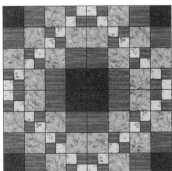

Pure red mini-4-patch block

Step 55

Step 56

Step 57

Step 58

Step 59

Step 60

Step 61

Watch how this quilt changes when red is added. Are the important parts of the quilt emphasized? Do you see how the Trip Around the World design is almost lost when you put such a warm color in these patches?

50 Find your very dark blue in the palette and click to replace the red. Watch how your quilt design changes.

51 Click the Paintbrush tool.

52 Click with red on one large center square.

53 Click Save in Sketchbook.

54 Use the Eyedropper tool to pick up your very dark blue somewhere on the quilt. Click with the Paintbrush tool and replace the red square.

55 Find red in the palette. Click with red on one of your medium blue mini-4-patch blocks.

56 Click Save in Sketchbook.

57 Go back to your all blue quilt by using the Eyedropper tool to pick up your medium blue somewhere on the quilt. Click with the Paintbrush tool and replace the mini-red square.

Notice how red is stronger than the blues. It advances on the quilt, even when used in small quantities.

4

Add Yellow to Your Quilt

58 Click the Swap tool.

59 Find a **pure bright yellow** in the palette and click to replace your palest blue.

60 Click Save in Sketchbook.

Notice how using yellow in the diamond accentuates the overall design just as red did.

61 Click the Paintbrush tool.

62 Click (without the CTRL key) to change the four dark blue center squares to this same yellow. Sit back and see how the yellow takes over the quilt.

63 Save this quilt in the Sketchbook.

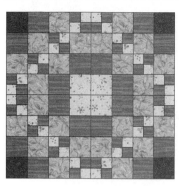

Step 63

Use All Three Primary Colors

64 In the mini-4-patch squares, CTRL + click to change the medium blue to **pure red**.

65 Click Save in Sketchbook.

66 Change the four center squares to red (without the CTRL key).

67 Click Save in Sketchbook.

68 Change the four outer corners to red.

69 Click Save in Sketchbook.

Step 62

Study your Quilts

•   Click the View Sketchbook button, then the Quilts tab. Use the arrows to flip through a slide show of the different versions of your Carrie Nation quilt.

•   Because color strikes you first, flipping quickly through your quilts makes it very clear which colors advance and which recede.

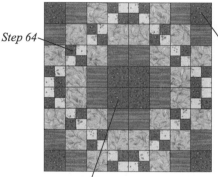

Step 64

Step 68

Step 66

Remember What You Practiced

•   The general Rule of Color Dominance:

> These colors dominate or advance — *Warm, pure, dark.*

> These colors recede or become background — *Cool, grayed tones, pale.*

•   This tendency to advance or recede is **relative**. Every time you put colors together in a new arrangement, you create different interactions in which the same colors may be stronger or weaker than before.

•   The amount of a color in a quilt also affects its strength.

Step 69   *View Sketchbook*

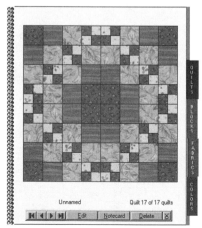

Unnamed   Quilt 17 of 17 quilts

View the quilts in your Sketchbook

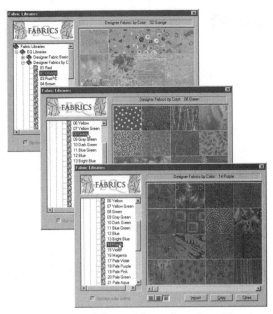

Try using many different fabrics from these libraries in your quilt to show even more color dominance

Suggestions for More Practice

- Click the View Sketchbook button, then the Quilts tab.

- Edit any of your quilts. See what happens when you replace a fabric with a more toned version of itself.

- Add one or more borders to this quilt.

- Edit any of your quilts and try practicing these same rules of color dominance, but with primary *and* secondary colors. Go to Libraries — Fabric Library — Designer Fabrics by Color, and copy some fabrics from orange, green, and purple/violet. Try using their values and tones as well.

4

Color Temperature is Relative

Color Theory

Remember that the cool colors are the blues and greens of the sky, sea, and grass. Warm colors are the reds, oranges, and yellows of fire and the sun.

When we refer to a color as warm or cool, it has this character in relation to other colors around it. Each time we choose a new set of fabrics, this relationship can change. The warmth of the fabrics we choose, and therefore their strength, is always affected by the surrounding colors.

Let's Play with Color Warmth

1   Start EQ5.

2   Choose Create a New Project.

3   Type the name for your new project:
    C Temp is Relative - Broken Sash.

4   Click OK.

5   Click Worktable — Work on Quilt.

Design the Quilt

Layout

6   Click Quilt — New Quilt — Horizontal.

7   Click the Layout tab along the bottom of the screen.

8   Under Number of blocks, click the arrows to read 4 Horizontal and 5 Vertical.

9   Under Size of blocks, drag the sliders to read 8.00 Width and 8.00 Height.

10 Under Sashing, drag the sliders to read 1.00 Width and 0.00 Height. Be sure Sash border is *not* checked (Clicking here will turn this check on and off.)

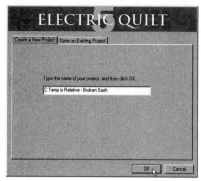

Steps 2-4

Step 6

Steps 8-10

Step 12

Step 14

Step 15

Step 17

Step 17

Step 18

Step 21

Step 22

Step 24

Border

11 Click the Borders tab along the bottom of the screen.

12 Click the Add button once to make a total of 2 borders.

13 Be sure there is a check next to All under Adjust Size. (Clicking will turn this check on and off.)

14 Click on the inner border. Drag one of the sliders to 1.00. All sides will adjust automatically.

15 Click on the outer border. Drag one of the sliders to read 3.00.

16 Click the Layer 1 tab along the bottom of the screen.

Blocks

17 Go to Libraries — Block Library — EQ Libraries — 2 Contemporary Pieced — Good Alternative Blocks.

18 Find and click on the Broken Sash Strip II block. (It is the third block from the end of this category.)

19 Click Copy. The block disappears temporarily, indicating you've copied it to your Sketchbook.

20 Click Close.

Fabrics

21 Click Libraries — Palette Library — My Palettes tab.

22 Find and click on your Pure Colors and Values palette.

23 Click Load.

24 Click "Delete all existing fabrics," then OK.

4

Blocks

25 Click the Set tool and then the Blocks tab of the palette.

26 Click on the Broken Sash Strip II block to select it.

27 Hold down your keyboard CTRL key and click in one of the large squares in your quilt layout. All squares will fill with the Broken Sash Strip II block.

Color Quilt 1

28 Click the Spraycan tool (not the EQ4 Spraycan tool). Click on the Solids tab. You will use four solid analogous colors for this quilt: red-violet, violet, blue-violet and blue.

29 Find **pure red-violet** and click on it. Hold down your keyboard CTRL key and click to make all the diamonds red-violet.

30 Click on a **pure violet**. CTRL + click on the sashing (narrow vertical stripes) and the inner border to color them all violet.

31 Click on **pure blue-violet**. CTRL + click to color all the wide vertical stripes blue-violet.

32 Click on **pure blue**. CTRL + click the triangles behind the red-violet diamonds. The triangles will all color at the same time.

33 CTRL + click on the outer border to color it **blue**.

34 Click the Save in Sketchbook button.

Look at the quilt. Notice how the diamonds stand out as a main design element. This is partly because of color: the red-violet is the warmest color in this set, and warm colors are stronger than cool. The violet stripes also stand out. This is because they are dark, and dark colors can be strong.

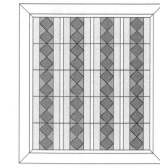

Step 25

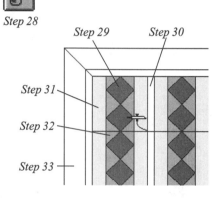

Step 27

Step 28

Step 29   *Step 30*

Step 31

Step 32

Step 33

Step 34

Final quilt design

4

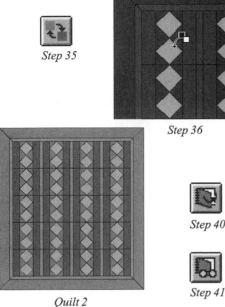

Step 35

Step 36

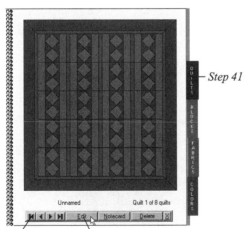

Quilt 2

Step 40

Step 41

Step 42   Step 43

Step 45

Color Quilt 2

35 Now, let's change the colors for Quilt 2. Click the Swap tool (not the EQ4 Swap tool).

36 Click on **pure yellow-orange**. Click on the red-violet diamonds in the quilt.

37 Click on **pure orange** and click on the inner border. The inner border and sash strips will change to orange.

38 Click on **pure red** and click the outer border. The outer border and triangles behind the diamonds will change to red.

39 Click on **pure red-violet** and click the wide vertical stripes.

40 Save Quilt 2 in the Sketchbook.

Look at Quilt 2. Notice what parts of the design stand out and how they are colored. Which colors in this set of four are strongest? The red-violet is now the coolest color in the quilt and has lost most of its power.

Quilts 3-6: Let's Use Prints and Add Variety

41 Click the View Sketchbook button and then the Quilts tab.

42 Use the first arrow to go to Quilt 1.

43 Click the Edit button. Let's use the same color combination as in Quilt 1, but with a variety of prints in different values and textures.

44 Make sure you are still using the Swap tool (not the EQ4 Swap tool).

45 Click on the Prints tab to see the fabrics available.

Step 41

4

46 Find a **red-violet print** in the palette and click to select it.

47 Click on the solid red-violet diamonds in the quilt. They will now change to a print.

48 Click on a **violet print** and click to replace the solid violet in the quilt.

49 Repeat Step 48 for **blue-violet** and **blue**.

50 Click the Save in Sketchbook button for this cool quilt in prints.

51 Click the Paintbrush tool. (The Paintbrush allows us to click one by one and add as much variety as possible.)

As you already know, CTRL + click replaces across the entire quilt at the same time. ALT + click, however, does this replacing to every other one. Using ALT + click to add variety slowly to your quilt, gives you the chance to do twice as much. Let's try it.

52 Click on a **different red-violet print** in the palette.

53 Hold down the ALT key on your keyboard and click on a red-violet diamond.

54 Choose a **third red-violet** and use ALT + click to color a different diamond.

55 Choose a **fourth red-violet** and use ALT + click to color yet another different diamond. (You may get more prints from the Fabric Library if you need to.)

56 Repeat this process of choosing a different print of the same color and using ALT + click to finish the rest of this quilt.

57 Save Quilt 4 in the Sketchbook.

Step 47

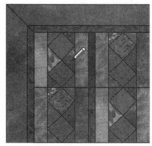

Step 49

Step 50   *Step 51*

Step 56

Step 57

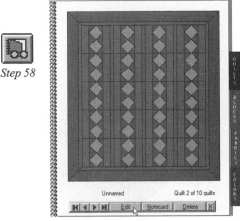

Step 58

Step 58-59

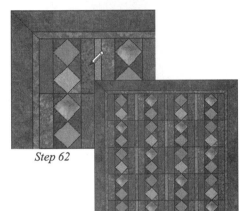

Step 62

Quilt 2

Step 63

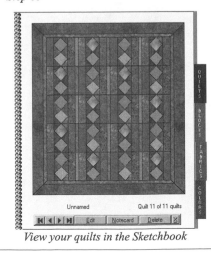

View your quilts in the Sketchbook

58 Click the View Sketchbook button and then the Quilts tab.

59 Find Quilt 2 and click the Edit button. Let's use the same color combination as in Quilt 2, but with a variety of prints in different values and textures.

60 Use any or several values of these colors: **red-violet**, **red**, **orange** and **yellow-orange**. Use the Swap tool initially to recolor the quilt in prints.

61 Save this warm quilt with prints in the Sketchbook.

62 Use the Paintbrush and ALT key to add variety and texture to your quilt as you did in Steps 52-56.

63 Save Quilt 6 in the Sketchbook.

Study your Broken Sash Quilts

• Click the View Sketchbook button, then the Quilts tab. Use the arrows to flip through a slide show of your quilts.

• You have played with one color, red-violet, and studied its relationship to its analogous colors. When placed with the cool colors, red-violet is warm and strong. But when placed with its warm neighbors, red-violet becomes the coolest and weakest color. This relationship between colors is always changing.

• When you colored your quilts, you did not use the red-violet in the outer border. Do you know why? The outer border is large and any color you place there will be strong simply because of quantity — when there is a lot of any color in a quilt, it becomes stronger. For this lesson, I did not want quantity to overcome color temperature.

4

Remember

- On the color wheel, we distinguish between the warm and the cool colors. But each time we put fabrics and the colors they contain together, we are creating new color relationships in which these colors may appear less cool or warm. It is all part of the fun of designing with color in mind.

- Warm colors are stronger than cool colors. Knowing this helps us control our quilt designs and which elements are seen first.

- You must analyze every set of fabrics you are considering for a project to know which colors are stronger.

- Where you put strong colors depends upon what part of the design you want to emphasize.

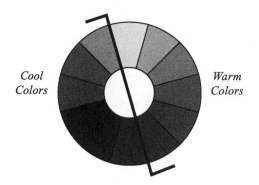

Cool Colors

Warm Colors

4

4

Understanding Simultaneous Contrast

Color Theory

Complements always go together and are harmonious. But they are so strong that we often balance them by using *unequal* amounts of each, letting one be the focus of the design and the other the accent.

The strong contrast that complements create when used together is called simultaneous contrast. They enhance and intensify each other and create an illusion of vibration. Simultaneous contrast is a powerful color scheme that guarantees a visually dramatic quilt.

It works best with pure colors and saturated values of pure colors (no grays allowed!). Grays should only be used to dilute simultaneous contrast.

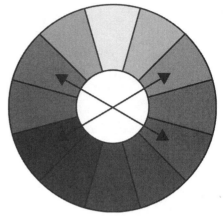

Complementary colors are ones opposite each other on the color wheel. This opposition creates vibration.

Let's Play with Simultaneous Contrast in Striped Quilts

1 Start EQ5.

2 Choose Create a New Project.

3 Type the name for your new project: C Simult Contrast - Vertical Bars.

4 Click OK.

5 Click Worktable — Work on Quilt.

Design the Quilt

Layout

6 Click Quilt — New Quilt — Horizontal.

7 Click the Layout tab along the bottom of the screen.

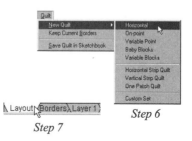

Steps 2-4

Step 7

Step 6

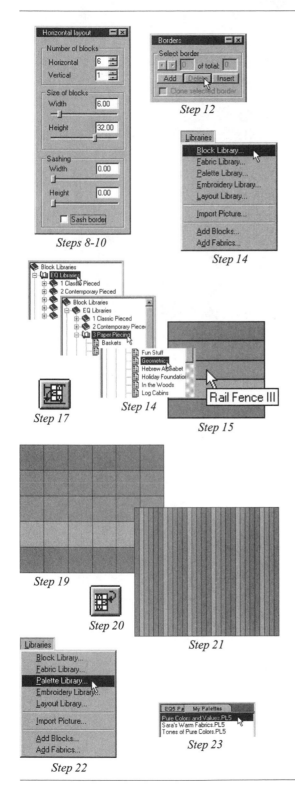

Steps 8-10

Step 12

Step 14

Step 14

Step 17

Step 15

Step 19

Step 20

Step 21

Step 22

Step 23

8 Under Number of blocks, click the arrows to read 6 Horizontal and 1 Vertical.

9 Under Size of blocks, drag the sliders to read 6.00 Width and 32.00 Height (this is not a typo!).

10 Under Sashing, drag both the sliders to read 0.00.

Borders

11 Click the Borders tab along the bottom of the screen.

12 Click the Delete button to eliminate borders.

13 Click the Layer 1 tab along the bottom of the screen.

Block

14 Click Libraries — Block Library — EQ Libraries — 3 Paper Piecing — Geometrics.

15 Find and click on the Rail Fence III block. It is the third block in the first column.

16 Click Copy; then Close.

17 Click the Set tool and then the Blocks tab.

18 Click on the Rail Fence III block to select it.

19 Hold down your keyboard CTRL key and click in the quilt. The Rail Fence III block will appear, looking like horizontal stripes.

20 Click the Rotate tool.

21 CTRL + click to rotate all the blocks once. Now your quilt is full of long, vertical stripes.

Collect the Fabrics for the Quilt

22 Click Libraries — Palette Library — My Palettes tab.

23 Click on the Pure Colors and Values palette to select it.

24 Click Load.

4

25 Choose "Delete all existing fabrics," and click OK.

26 Click the Paintbrush tool and then the Solids tab. Scroll through the solids to remind yourself of the colors available.

Tip ———————————————

Remember that you can add values and tones for any swatch by right-clicking on it.

Quilt 1: Complements Red and Green

You are now ready to play with simultaneous contrast. Use CTRL + click for all colorings in this lesson.

27 Find a **pure red** and CTRL + click on the far-left stripe. Notice that every sixth stripe changes to red at the same time.

28 Find a **dark rich red** and CTRL + click it into the second stripe.

29 In the third stripe, CTRL + click in a **pure green**.

30 In the fourth stripe, CTRL + click in a **darker value of green**.

31 In the fifth stripe, CTRL + click in a **dark green**.

32 Save the Red and Green Simultaneous Stripes quilt in your Sketchbook.

Sit back and look at your quilt. It should almost vibrate or wave as you stare at it. This is simultaneous contrast. The slight gradations in value enhance this illusion.

Quilt 2: Red-violet and Yellow-green

33 Follow Steps 27-31 to color this quilt. Color the stripes from left to right:

Three values of **red-violet** (one pure, one dark, and one other)

Two values of **yellow-green** (one pure and one dark).

34 Save Quilt 2 in the Sketchbook.

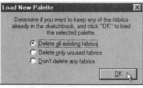

Step 25

Step 26

Complements Red and Green

Step 32

Complements Red-violet and Yellow-green

Step 34

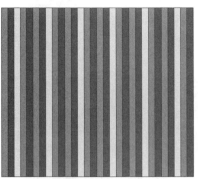

Complements using 2 Red-violets and 3 Yellow-greens

Step 36

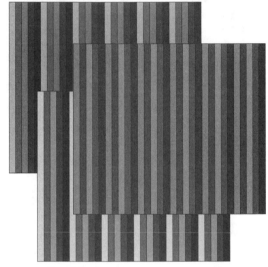

Step 37 - Simultaneous contrast quilts

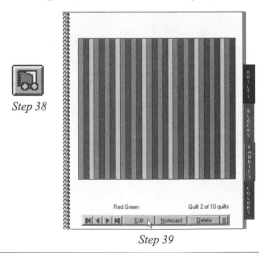

Step 38

Step 39

35 Try making a variation of this quilt. Use two values of **red-violet** and three of **yellow-green**.

36 Save this quilt in the Sketchbook.

Color Quilts Using Other Complementary Pairs of Colors

37 Color other simultaneous contrast quilts, following Steps 27-36 for these color schemes:

Orange and blue

Yellow-orange and blue-violet

Red-orange and blue-green

Study your Simultaneous Contrast Striped Quilts

• Click the View Sketchbook button, then the Quilts tab. Use the arrows to scroll through the quilts from first to last.

• This should be a visually overwhelming quilt show: powerful quilts full of complementary pairs of pure colors.

• In each quilt, you used one pair of complements, but also their values. Check whether quantity (the set of three) helps the cool section be stronger.

How to Soften or Dilute Complementary Contrast

What if you don't want such a strong contrast but want to keep the basic color scheme? Any medium value of gray will soften simultaneous contrast. Try adding gray to one or two of your quilts.

38 Click the View Sketchbook button then the Quilts tab.

39 Find your red and green quilt in the Sketchbook and click the Edit button.

4

40 Change one row only into a **medium gray**. Put the gray into an outside row of the set of three. This way it will be in between the complements and act as a buffer.

41 Save this quilt in the Sketchbook.

42 Repeat Steps 38-40 with one or more quilts. Save each quilt in the Sketchbook.

Study All of Your Simultaneous Contrast Quilts and Remember

- Remind yourself of how simultaneous contrast works. Use the pure colors of two complements to intensify each other and create the illusion of vibration.

- You can avoid simultaneous contrast by using gray to tone down the quilt. Or, you can use its potential for creating dynamite quilts.

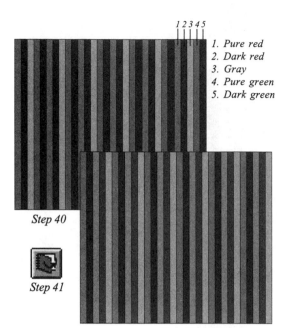

1 2 3 4 5

1. Pure red
2. Dark red
3. Gray
4. Pure green
5. Dark green

Step 40

Step 41

Step 42

Fail-Safe Color Schemes

Chapter 5

Analyzing Color Contrast Within Fabrics

Color Theory

Fabric designers use color theory to design beautiful fabrics. A "line" of fabric will contain a variety of fabric prints and of color combinations. These range from one-color color schemes to busy, multi-colored color schemes.

Quilters often use a multi-colored fabric as their theme fabric, using the color scheme within the fabric to choose other fabrics that are guaranteed to go together. It is logical: If the fabric designer followed color theory in designing her fabrics and considered this color combination a good one, then I can assume it will make a good quilt. And the assumption is correct. Color theory offers you Tried and True Color schemes to play with.

Let's look closely at some fabrics and see exactly what is going on within them color-wise.

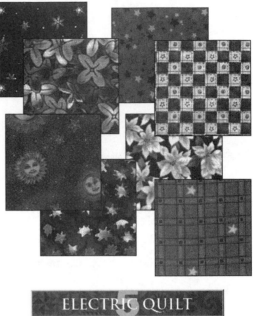

Explore Color Contrast

1   Start EQ5.

2   Choose Create a New Project.

3   Type the name for your new project:
C Color Contrast Within Fabrics.

4   Click OK.

5   Click Worktable — Work on Quilt.

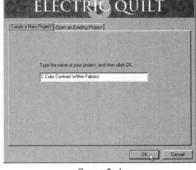

Steps 2-4

Design the Quilt

Layout

6   Click Quilt — New Quilt — Horizontal.

7   Click the Layout tab along the bottom of the screen.

8   Under Number of blocks, click the arrows to read 2 Horizontal and 3 Vertical.

9   Under Size of blocks, drag the sliders to read 12.00 Width and 12.00 Height.

10 Under Sashing, drag both the sliders to read 0.00.

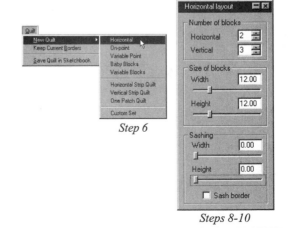

Step 6

Steps 8-10

Borders

11 Click the Borders tab along the bottom of the screen.

12 Click the Delete button, so you have no border.

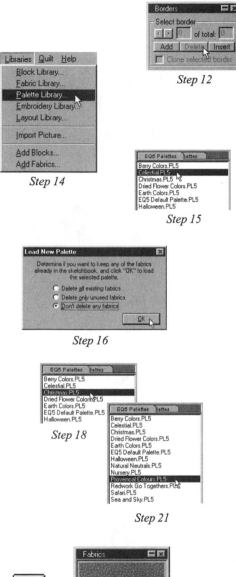

Step 12

13 Click the Layer 1 tab along the bottom of the screen.

Collect Fabrics

14 We will keep the EQ5 default palette and load three other palettes. Click Libraries — Palette Library — EQ5 Palettes.

Step 14

15 Click on the Celestial palette and click Load.

Step 15

16 Choose "Don't delete any fabrics," then click OK.

17 Click Libraries — Palette Library — EQ5 Palettes again.

Step 16

18 Click on the Christmas palette and click Load.

19 Choose "Don't delete any fabrics," and click OK.

20 Click Libraries — Palette Library — EQ5 Palettes.

Step 18

21 Click on the Provencal Colours palette and click Load.

22 Choose "Don't delete any fabrics," and click OK.

Step 21

Enlarge the Palette

The six-block quilt fills the entire left side of the screen. Let's enlarge the palette so it fills the rest of the screen. This will make it much easier to see the actual colors in the fabrics.

23 Click the Paintbrush tool; then the Prints tab.

Step 23

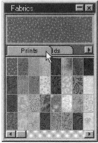

Step 23

5

24 Place your cursor over the top-left corner of the Fabrics palette until your cursor changes into a double-sided diagonal arrow.

25 Click and drag the outer border up and to the left until it almost touches the quilt. Notice that the space on the top of the palette that shows the chosen fabric is now quite large. This will make it easy for you to see the colors and patterns in the print.

26 If necessary, do the same thing to the bottom-right corner, by pulling down and right to make your palette as large as possible.

Pull corner up and to the left

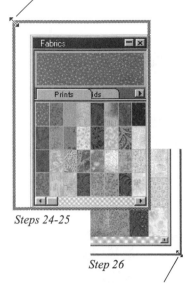

Steps 24-25

Step 26

Pull corner down and to the right

Tip
When you are analyzing a print, click on it so it becomes the focused fabric at the top of the palette. Now that you are seeing a much larger swatch, you can analyze the colors and pattern better. The print is only selected, whether you color with it or not after that is up to you.

Find Six Fabrics That Contain Several Values of Only One Color
Look at the quilt design. It is simply six squares. You are going to find six examples of one-color fabrics containing several values.

27 Hold your cursor over a fabric in the palette and the name of the fabric will appear.

28 Look in your prints at the first palette group, which is the EQ palette, by scrolling all the way to the left. Find and click on a pink fabric called: The Cabbage Rose Collection by Barbara Brandeburg. Notice how the fabric is one color, but contains light and dark values of that color.

29 Click this fabric into one of the squares of your quilt.

30 Scroll through the palette and click on any other fabric that looks like it might fit this description.

31 Examine it now that it is the focus fabric.

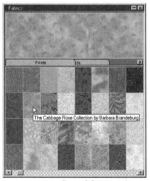

Step 28

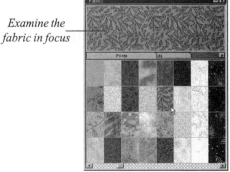

Examine the fabric in focus

Step 31

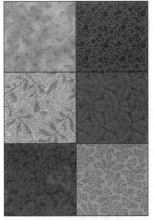

Step 33

Step 34

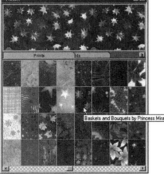

Step 35

Step 37

32 Click it into the quilt if it is a one-color print. If not, try to find a fabric that is a one-color print with several values.

33 Repeat Steps 28-30 for five more fabrics.

34 Save your one-color fabrics quilt in the Sketchbook.

Tip

In the next quilts we will be using the same quilt layout, but different fabrics each time. If you want to start with a plain quilt each time, just click the Solids tab of the Fabrics palette. Click on white and CTRL + click it into your quilt. Then click the Prints tab to continue with the next quilt of contrasting fabrics.

Find Six Fabrics That Contain Analogous Colors

35 Look in your prints at the Celestial palette (second palette group). Find and click on a dark violet fabric with stars called: Baskets and Bouquets by Princess Mirah.

36 Click this fabric into one of the squares of your quilt. Notice how the fabric contains both violet and red-violet, which are beside each other on the color wheel.

37 Follow Steps 28-30, filling your quilt with fabrics that contain analogous contrast. Refer to the color wheel on page 17 if necessary.

38 Click the Save in Sketchbook button.

39 You may want to make another quilt that contains analogous fabrics, since you will find that there are many fabrics in the palette that use this color scheme.

Step 38

40 Click the Save in Sketchbook button to save your second analogous colors quilt.

5

Find Six Fabrics That Contain Warm-Cool Contrast

41 Look in your prints at the Provencal Colours palette (last palette group). Find and click on a red fabric with white polka dots and blue flowers called: Cherry Berry Chicken by Sharon Yenter.

42 Click this fabric into one of the squares of your quilt. Notice how the fabric contains both cool color and warm colors.

43 Follow Steps 28-30, filling your quilt with fabrics that contain one warm and one cool color. You will find many that do. Remember warm colors are reds, yellows, and oranges, while cool colors are blues, greens and violets.

44 Click the Save in Sketchbook button.

Find Six Fabrics That Contain Complementary Contrast

45 Find and click on a red and green plaid fabric from the Christmas palette called: Country Christmas by Barri Gaudet.

46 Click this fabric into one of the squares of your quilt.

47 Follow Steps 28-30, filling your quilt with fabrics that contain two complements. They may have another color, probably a neutral, but stick to predominantly two-color prints.

48 Click the Save in Sketchbook button.

Find Six Fabrics That Contain Lots of Colors

49 Look in the Celestial palette for a dark blue fabric with many-colored fireworks called: Celebrate by Hoffman.

50 Click this fabric into one of the squares of your quilt.

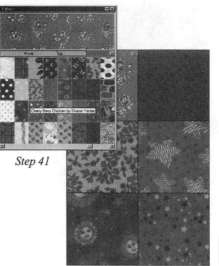

Step 41

Step 43   *Step 44*

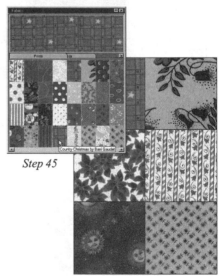

Step 45

Step 47

Step 48

Step 49

5

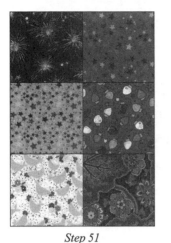

Step 52

Step 51

View the quilts in your Sketchbook

51 Follow Steps 28-30, filling your quilt with other busy, many-colored fabrics.

52 Click the Save in Sketchbook button.

Study your Fabric Sets & Remember What You Learned

• Click the View Sketchbook button, then the Quilts tab. Use the arrows to flip through a slide show of fabric contrasts.

• Remember that fabric designers use color theory to design beautiful fabrics, and you can use the same combinations to design beautiful quilts.

• Consider using a many-colored fabric as your source for choosing the colors in your next quilt. We will experiment with this concept later in this chapter.

5

Geometric Shapes Create Color Schemes

Color Theory

Certain color combinations create successful quilts. Here's a "formula" you can use to find one of these winning color combinations: Place a certain geometric shape (a square or triangle) on top of the color wheel. Note the colors at the shape's corners. These colors will automatically give you a wonderful and unusual color scheme. In this lesson you will use this "formula" to collect and organize several sets of these harmonious colors and play with them a bit.

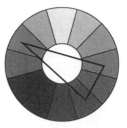

Use the corners of a triangle to find a color scheme

Let's Play with Color Combinations

1 Start EQ5.

2 Choose Create a New Project.

3 Type the name for your new project: C Geometric Shapes - Wedding Ring.

4 Click OK.

5 Click Worktable — Work on Quilt.

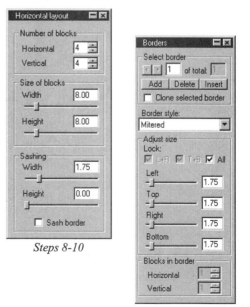

Steps 2-4

Design Charts of the Color Formulas

Layout

6 Click Quilt — New Quilt — Horizontal.

7 Click the Layout tab.

8 Under Number of blocks, click the arrows to read 4 Horizontal and 4 Vertical.

9 Under Size of blocks, drag the sliders to read 8.00 Width and 8.00 Height.

10 Under Sashing, drag the sliders to read 1.75 Width and 0.00 Height. Be sure Sash border is *not* checked.

Borders

11 Click the Borders tab.

12 Be sure there is a check next to All under Adjust Size.

13 Drag one of the sliders to read 1.75. All borders will adjust automatically.

Steps 8-10

Steps 12-13

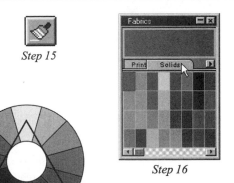

Step 15

Step 16

*Equilateral Triangle
Color Combinations*

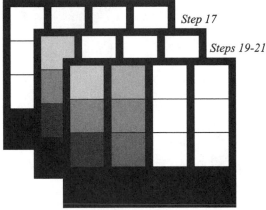

Step 17

Steps 19-21

Step 22

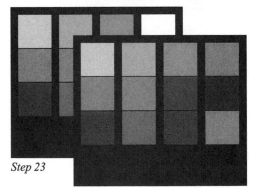

Step 23

Step 24

Step 25

Color the Charts

14 Click the Layer 1 tab.

15 Click the Paintbrush tool.

16 Click the Solids tab. You are going to use solids for the charts.

Chart 1: Equilateral Triangle Color Combinations

17 Click on **black** and click on the four squares in the bottom row of the quilt. Then, CTRL + click black into the three strips of sashing and the border. These will provide visual space between the four color schemes.

18 Begin with the four color combinations dictated by an equilateral triangle. Color the chart from left to right, putting a different color combination in each column.

19 The first set of three colors make the primary colors. Click on **pure yellow**; then click it into the top square in the first (left) column.

20 Click on **pure red**; then click it into the second square in the first column.

21 Click on **pure blue**; then click it into the third square in the first column.

22 Repeat Steps 19-21, putting **yellow-orange**, **red-violet** and **blue-green** into the 2nd column.

23 Repeat Steps 19-21, putting the secondary colors – **orange**, **violet** and **green** – into the 3rd column.

24 Repeat Steps 19-21, putting **red-orange**, **blue-violet** and **yellow-green** into the 4th column.

25 Save Chart 1 in the Sketchbook.

5

26 Open the Sketchbook and label the chart: Equilateral Triangle Harmonies. To do this, click the Notecard button, next to Name, and then click the X in the upper right corner to close the Notecard.

27 Close the Sketchbook with the X in the lower-right corner.

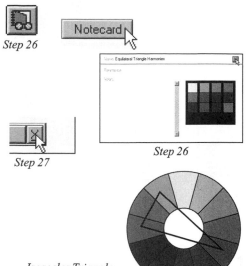

Step 26

Step 27

Step 26

Chart 2: Three Corners of an Isosceles Triangle

28 Repeat Steps 19-27, this time using an isosceles triangle. Fill four columns with four sets of three pure colors. There are actually twelve different combinations dictated by an isosceles triangle, but four will give you the idea. Use these sets:

29 Column 1: **yellow**, **red-violet** and **blue-violet**.

30 Column 2: **red-orange**, **blue** and **green**.

31 Column 3: **blue-violet**, **yellow** and **orange**.

32 Column 4: **red**, **blue-green** and **yellow-green**.

33 Save the quilt in the Sketchbook.

34 Label the Chart: Isosceles Triangle Harmonies.

Chart 3: Four Corners of a Square

35 Repeat Steps 19-27, filling three columns with three sets of four pure colors. There are only three combinations dictated by a square, so the last column will be black:

36 Column 1: **yellow**, **red-orange**, **violet** and **blue-green**.

37 Column 2: **yellow-orange**, **red**, **blue-violet** and **green**.

38 Column 3: **orange**, **red-violet**, **blue** and **yellow-green**.

39 Column 4: color the squares in this 4th column **black**.

Isosceles Triangle Color Combinations

Steps 29-32

Step 33

Name Isosceles Triangle Harmonies

Reference

Notes

Step 34

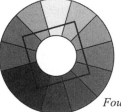

Four Corners of a Square

5

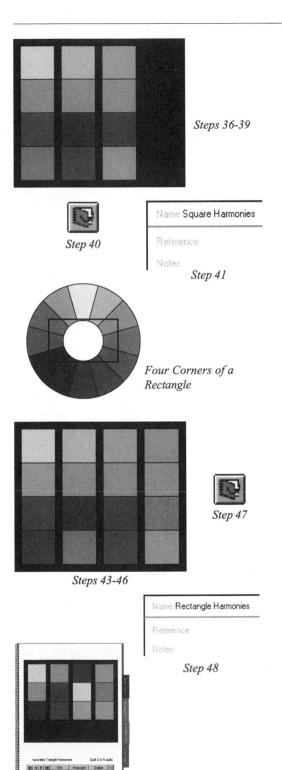

Steps 36-39

Step 40

Name Square Harmonies

Reference

Notes

Step 41

*Four Corners of a
Rectangle*

Step 47

Steps 43-46

Name Rectangle Harmonies

Reference

Notes

Step 48

Study the Charts

40 Save the quilt in the Sketchbook.

41 Label the Chart: Square Harmonies.

Chart 4: Four Corners of a Rectangle

42 Repeat Steps 19-27, filling four columns with four sets of four pure colors. There are six combinations dictated by a rectangle, but four will give you the idea:

43 Column 1: **yellow**, **orange**, **violet** and **blue**.

44 Column 2: **yellow-orange**, **red-orange**, **blue-violet** and **blue-green**.

45 Column 3: **orange**, **red**, **blue** and **green**.

46 Column 4: **red-orange**, **red-violet**, **blue-green** and **yellow-green**.

47 Save the quilt in the Sketchbook.

48 Label the Chart: Rectangle Harmonies.

Study the Charts to See What Colors Go Together

• Click the View Sketchbook button and then the Quilts tab.

• Use the arrows to flip through the Color Combination Charts.

• Look at all of these guaranteed harmonious color combination. See how practically every color goes with every other color! That is the lesson to remember when playing with color: just play, enjoy and experiment with new color combinations. If you like them, great (and they probably technically go together via some formula). If you are like most of us, you work in your favorite colors. When you want to expand your repertoire, however, these formulas can give you the confidence to plan quilts around what you may consider unusual color combinations. Let's try a few right now. You will be surprised at how dramatic they can be!

5

Let's Design Some Quilts

Layout

49 Click Quilt — New Quilt — Horizontal.

50 Click the Layout tab.

51 Under Number of blocks, click the arrows to read 4 Horizontal and 4 Vertical.

52 Under Size of blocks, drag the sliders to read 12.00 Width and 12.00 Height.

53 Under Sashing, drag both sliders to read 0.00 to eliminate the sashing.

Border

54 Click the Borders tab along the bottom of the screen.

55 Be sure there is a check next to All under Adjust Size. (Clicking will turn this check on and off.)

56 Click Add to create a total of 2 borders.

57 Click on the inner border and drag one of the sliders to 4.00. All sides will adjust automatically.

58 Click on the outer border and drag one of the sliders to 1.00.

59 Click the Layer 1 tab.

Block

60 Click Libraries — Block Library — EQ Libraries — 1 Classic Pieced — Classics.

61 Drag the horizontal scrollbar below the block to the right to see all the blocks in this book.

62 Position your cursor over a block and the block name appears. You want to find the Double Wedding Ring block.

63 Click on the Double Wedding Ring block to select it. You'll see a frame around it to know it's the selected one.

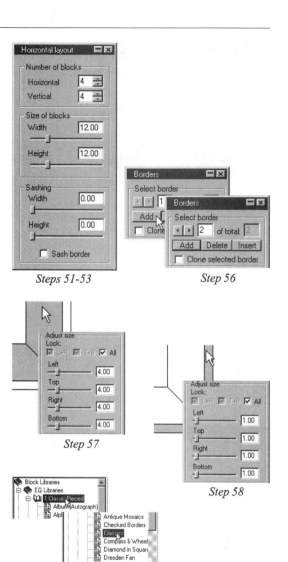

Steps 51-53　　　*Step 56*

Step 57

Step 58

Step 60

Steps 62-63

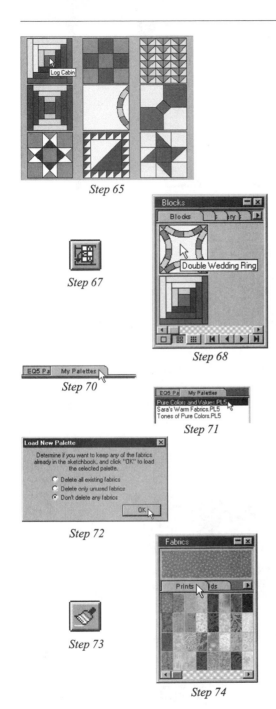

Step 65

Step 67

Step 68

Step 70

Step 71

Step 72

Step 73

Step 74

64 Click Copy. You'll notice that the block temporarily disappears, indicating you've "copied" it into your Sketchbook.

65 Find and click on the Log Cabin block and click Copy.

66 Click Close.

67 Click the Set tool.

68 Click on the Double Wedding Ring block to select it.

69 Position your cursor over any block space in your empty quilt layout. Hold down your keyboard CTRL key and click. All blocks are now filled with the Double Wedding Ring.

Collect the Fabrics for the Quilt

70 Click Libraries — Palette Library — My Palettes.

71 Click on the Pure Colors and Values Palette and click Load.

72 Choose "Don't delete any fabrics," then click OK.

73 Click the Paintbrush tool.

74 Click the Prints tab and scroll through it to see the wealth of colors available.

Color Quilt 1: Equilateral Triangle Formula of 3 Colors, The Primary Colors —Yellow, Red and Blue

75 Look at the quilt design, which is full of overlapping circles. Color the quilt as you want to. I suggest trying to emphasize the overlapping areas.

5

76 Use the primary colors: **yellow, red and blue**. Include a variety of prints, values and tones. In other words, use light yellows, pure yellows, dark yellows, and dull or drab yellows; then do the same with red and blue. You don't have to use them all, but use many or few of the prints, values and tones in such a way that you emphasize the overlapping circles. Color the borders with fabrics from the quilt center, using colors that enhance the color contrast. Do several versions of the quilt with different border treatments.

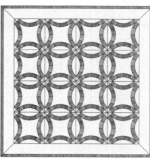

Step 77

Step 76

77 Save each of the quilts in the Sketchbook.

Color Quilt 2: Equilateral Triangle Formula of 3 Colors: Orange, Violet and Green

Repeat Steps 75 – 77, using the set of secondary colors.

Color Quilt 3: Isosceles Triangle Formula of 3 Colors: Yellow, Red-violet and Blue-violet

Repeat Steps 75 – 77.

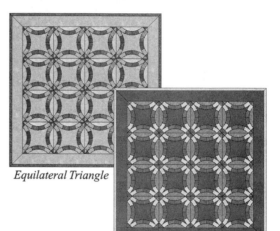
Equilateral Triangle

Isosceles Triangle

Try Some Log Cabin Quilts

The classic Log Cabin block, with its strip design, lends itself to playing with sets of four colors. Use the Set tool and CTRL + click the Log Cabin into the center of your existing quilt. If you like, use the Swap tool to speed up your coloring process. Try several of the formulas below for dramatic color schemes. Use bright, pure and dark colors and a variety of prints:

Square Formula:

Yellow, red-orange, violet and blue-green

Yellow-green, orange, red-violet and blue

Rectangle Formula:

Orange, violet, blue and yellow

Blue-violet, blue-green, yellow-orange and red-orange

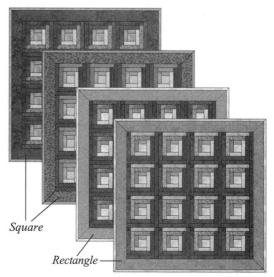
Square

Rectangle

5

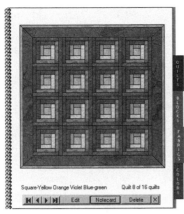

Square-Yellow Orange Violet Blue-green   Quilt 8 of 16 quilts

Study Your Quilts

Study Your Quilts and Remember what you Practiced

- Click the View Sketchbook button, then the Quilts tab. Use the arrows to flip through the quilts you designed.

- In each quilt, notice which colors advance or recede and ask yourself why.

- Notice how much of each color you used.

- Ask yourself whether the quilt is pleasing and why.

- Decide what color schemes you like or how you can change them to be more pleasing.

- Remember . . . that are many harmonious color combinations you may not have tried, so try them.

5

Split Complementary Colors

Color Theory

A tried and true formula for creating great color schemes grows out of what we know about complementary colors. Remember that complements always go together and are harmonious.

To define a split complementary color scheme, choose any color, find the complement, and then choose the two colors to either side of that complement. The three colors of a split complementary color scheme are actually the corners dictated by an Isosceles Triangle as we learned in the previous lesson. Together, these three colors form a gorgeous color scheme that is always harmonious.

Finished Split Complementary Quilt

Let's Play with Split Complementary Color Schemes

1   Start EQ5.

2   Choose Create a New Project.

3   Type the name for your new project:
C Split Complements - 4 Compasses.

4   Click OK.

5   Click Worktable — Work on Quilt.

Design the Quilt

Layout

6   Click Quilt — New Quilt — Horizontal.

7   Click the Layout tab along the bottom of the screen.

8   Under Number of blocks, click the arrows to read 2 Horizontal and 2 Vertical.

9   Under Size of blocks, drag the sliders to read 12.00 Width and 12.00 Height.

10 Under Sashing, drag both sliders to read 0.00 to eliminate the sashing.

Steps 2-4

Steps 8-10

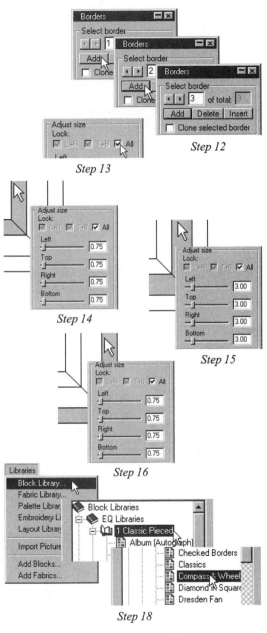

Step 12

Step 13

Step 14

Step 15

Step 16

Step 18

Step 19

Borders

11 Click the Borders tab along the bottom of the screen.

12 Click the Add button twice to make a total of three borders.

13 Be sure there is a check next to All under Adjust Size. (Clicking will turn this check on and off.)

14 Click on the inner border. Drag a slider to 0.75. All sides will adjust automatically.

15 Click on the middle border. Drag one of the sliders to 3.00. All sides will adjust automatically.

16 Click on the outer border. Drag a slider to 0.75. All sides will adjust automatically.

17 Click the Layer 1 tab along the bottom of the screen.

Block

18 Click Libraries — Block Library — EQ Libraries — 1 Classic Pieced — Compass & Wheels.

19 Find and click on the Mariner's Compass block. You want the Mariner's Compass with a blue background split into triangles.

20 Click Copy. You'll notice that the block temporarily disappears, indicating you've "copied" it into your Sketchbook.

21 Click Close.

22 Now you're back to the quilt worktable and ready to set blocks.

5

23 Click the Set tool. The Blocks palette will appear showing the Mariner's Compass block.

24 Click on the block to select it.

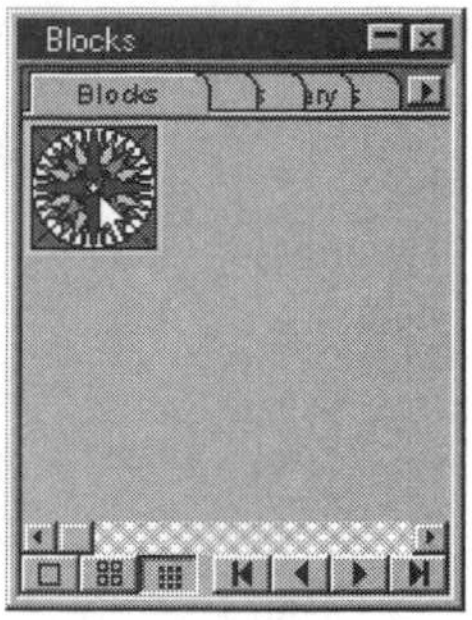

25 Hold down the CTRL key on your keyboard and click over any block in your empty quilt layout. The Mariner's Compass block now fills the quilt.

Select Fabrics for the Quilt

26 Click Libraries — Palette Library.

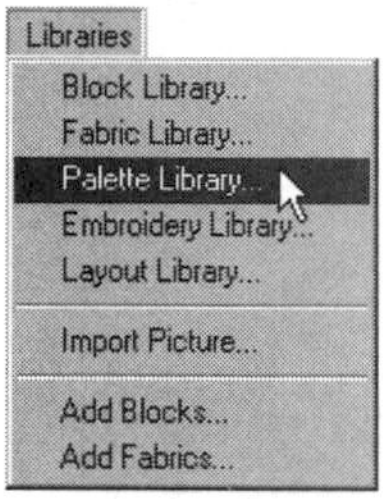

27 Click on the My Palettes tab behind the EQ5 Palettes tab.

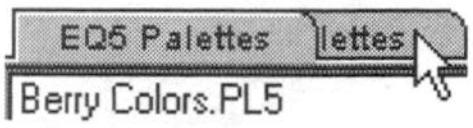

28 Choose Pure Colors and Values palette.

29 Click the Load button.

30 Click on "Don't delete any fabrics," then OK.

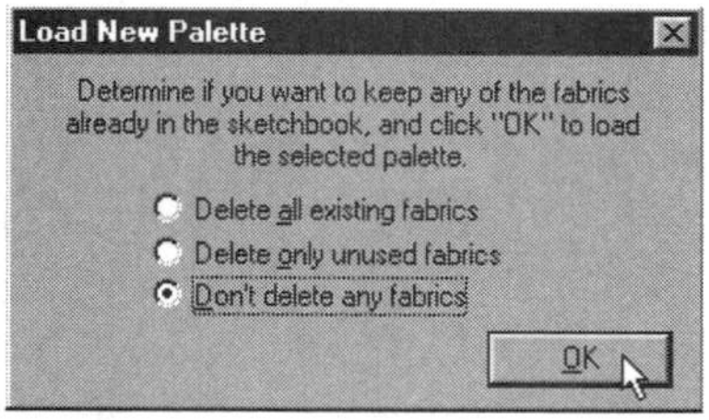

31 Click the Paintbrush tool and the palette will appear on the right of the screen.

32 Click the Prints tab on the Palette. Scroll to the right to see the fabrics available.

Tip

Have the color wheel available to refer to as you work.

Color Quilt 1

33 Let's begin with the yellow split complementary color scheme. On the color wheel, you can see that the complement of yellow is violet. The colors on either side of violet are blue-violet and red-violet. These two colors join the yellow to make a wonderful color scheme.

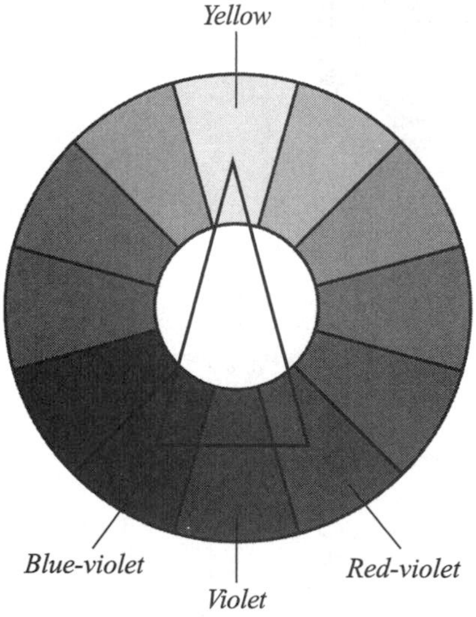

Step 23

Step 24

Step 27

Step 26

Step 28

Step 30

Yellow

Blue-violet

Violet

Red-violet

5

Steps 34-36

Step 36

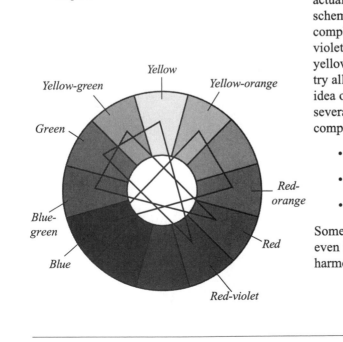

34 Now look at the quilt. The Mariner's Compass with its three layers of spokes and divided background spaces is perfect for playing with three colors. You can color the blocks in any way you want but remember several things:

- You are playing with warm and cool colors, which have different strengths

- Use a variety of values of any or all the colors

- Use the colors unequally (just as you would complements)

- Try to emphasize the wheel

35 Use the three borders to emphasize different colors. For each quilt, save several border colorations. These will be useful as you review your Sketchbook.

36 Save several quilts in the Sketchbook.

Color Several Quilts in Split Complementary Color Schemes

While there are only 6 complements, there are actually twelve split complementary color schemes. For instance, yellow and violet are complements, but you could use a yellow, blue-violet, red-violet theme or a yellow-orange, yellow-green, violet theme. You may not want to try all 12 in this lesson, but do enough to get the idea of how they work. I suggest you at least try several variations of each of these split complementary color sets:

- Red, blue-green and yellow-green

- Red-violet, green and yellow

- Blue, yellow-orange and red-orange

Some you may not like as well as others, but even if they are not your favorites, they are harmonious.

5

Study Your Quilts to See How Split Complementary Contrast Works

- Click the View Sketchbook button and then the Quilts tab. Use the arrows to flip through the saved quilts in order from first to last.

- Notice how different the compasses look and ask yourself why.

- Look at the backgrounds and see which are successful and ask why.

- Notice how different borders change the look of the quilt and ask why.

Remember What You Practiced

- In using the color wheel you can find new and often untried color schemes.

- Control what part of the design stands out by your placement of warm and cool colors.

- Use the border as an integral part of the quilt to emphasize what the viewer sees.

Suggestions for More Practice with Split Complements

- Do more quilts using the other split complementary color combinations. schemes.

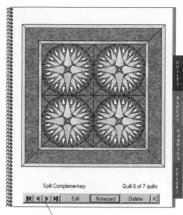

Study Your Quilts

5

Getting Your Color Scheme from Multi-colored Prints

Color Theory

You can use a wonderful, multi-colored print as the color "theme" for your quilt. Experienced artists, who design these prints, use color theory in designing their fabric's beautiful color schemes. So, identifying and using individual colors from the print guarantee you a harmonious color scheme in your quilt.

Seeing the individual colors in a busy print and selecting fabrics that match these colors are skills that sometimes take practice. Try going through the process of coordinating fabrics in this lesson.

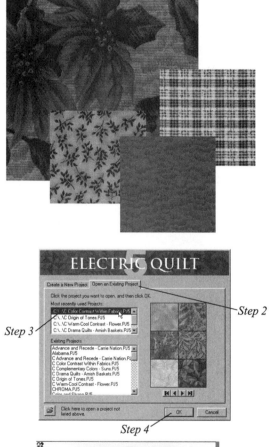

Let's Play with Theme Fabrics

1   Start EQ5.

2   Choose Open an Existing Project.

3   Click on the name of the project in the Most recently used Projects or Existing Projects list: C Color Contrast within Fabrics.

4   Click OK. Your Sketchbook will appear.

5   Click the Quilts tab.

6   Use the arrows to scroll to find the last quilt you made with six fabrics that contain lots of colors.

7   Click the Edit button to place it on the quilt worktable.

8   Look at these six prints you found in a previous lesson. If you identify the colors used to build these multi-colored prints, you would have six new color schemes to play with.

Let's start a new quilt and use one of these prints to see if we can find the colors the designer chose.

Step 2

Step 3

Step 4

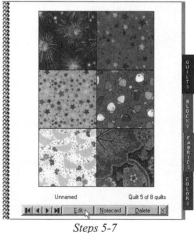

Steps 5-7

5

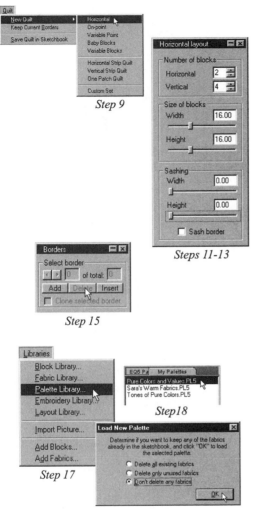

Step 9

Steps 11-13

Step 15

Step 18

Step 17

Step 20

Design the Layout for Your Fabric Sets

Layout

9 Click Quilt — New Quilt — Horizontal.

10 Click the Layout tab along the bottom of the screen.

11 Under Number of blocks, click the arrows to read 2 Horizontal and 4 Vertical.

12 Under Size of blocks, drag the sliders to read 16.00 Width and 16.00 Height.

13 Under Sashing, drag both the sliders to read 0.00 to eliminate the sashing.

Borders

14 Click the Borders tab along the bottom of the screen.

15 Click the Delete button to eliminate the border.

16 Click the Layer 1 tab along the bottom of the screen.

Collect More Prints

17 Click Libraries — Palette Library — My Palettes tab.

18 Click on the Pure Colors and Values palette.

19 Click Load.

20 Choose "Don't delete any fabrics," and click OK.

5

21 Click Libraries — Fabric Library — EQ Libraries — Designer Fabric Basics.

22 Go to Hoffman I. Scroll to the end of this category. Copy any two multi-colored, tie-dye prints.

23 Go to Hoffman II. Copy two or three multi-colored prints from this category.

24 Go to Maywood. Scroll to the end of this category. Copy any two flowery, multi-colored prints.

25 Click Close.

Build the Color Schemes

You are ready to create color schemes. Look at your quilt. It is simply eight squares. Use multi-colored prints from any palette, but try to find the coordinating fabrics from your Pure Colors and Values palette only.

26 Click the Paintbrush tool, then the Prints tab.

27 Find the **blue paisley print** named Turkish Treasures by P & B Textiles in the Provencal Colours palette.

28 CTRL + click to put this multi-colored blue paisley print into all squares. Look closely at the colors within the fabric and analyze their characteristics.

29 Find a **dark blue** in your Pure Colors and Values palette, and click it into one of the squares in the right column. Does this print work with this "theme" fabric?

Step 21

Step 21

Step 22

Step 23

Step 26

Step 27

Steps 28-29

5

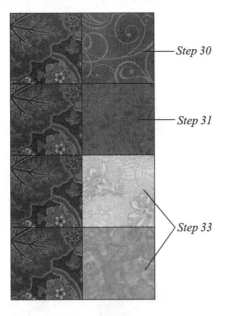

Step 30

Step 31

Step 33

Step 34

Steps 36-37

30 Find a **dark blue-violet** in your Pure Colors and Values palette, and click to replace the dark blue.

31 Find **dark blue-green** in your Pure Colors and Values palette, and click it into a different square in the right column.

32 Find a **dark yellow-orange** and a **red-orange tint**. Put these in the remaining two squares.

33 Change the patterns or values of the 4 coordinating prints until you find a pleasing combination.

34 Click Save in Sketchbook. You have just analyzed a print to find its composite colors.

35 Scroll through the palette and find another multi-colored print.

36 CTRL + click to fill all the squares of the quilt.

37 Find four fabrics that either match exactly or go with the colors in the **theme fabric**. As you find one, click it into one of the squares in the right column. If it doesn't look right, try another version of the color. Do strive to include a variety of values and, if possible, of pattern styles.

38 When you have chosen four fabrics, sit back and study the fabric set.

Do the colors seem to blend?

Did you include variety in value?

5

39 If you are satisfied, save it in your Sketchbook. If not, replace fabrics until you think the set looks good. There is no right answer.

Step 39

40 Choose a different theme fabric and follow Steps 35-39 to create more color schemes. Be sure you first CTRL + click to fill all squares with the theme fabric. You are trying to see color, and the very different leftover colors from the set before would make this difficult if you do not use CTRL + click first.

I recommend creating at least 8 color schemes. Some theme fabrics will be more difficult than others. But remember, you don't have to **like** the fabric or the colors to **learn** the process of "seeing."

Create many theme fabric sets

Study your Color Schemes

• Click the View Sketchbook button, then the Quilts tab. Use the arrows to scroll through the fabric sets from first to last. (Remember you opened your Color Contrast within Fabrics project, so you will have those quilts at the very beginning.)

• At a glance, you can see whether a color scheme you created from a multi-colored print contains contrast and variety.

• Notice how different each set is.

Remember

• You have practiced using one fabric to create a color scheme. Try this with your fabric collection, too, and with the bolts in quilt shops.

• If a color scheme is successful in a fabric, chances are it will be successful in a quilt. Use what a fabric artist already coordinated!

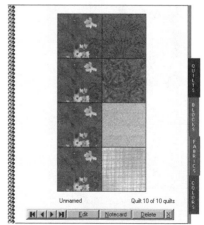

View your Sketchbook and study the coordinating fabrics

5

CHAPTER 5
Geometric Shapes Create Color Schemes

The points of an equilateral triangle create a red, yellow, blue harmony

An isosceles triangle creates a split-complementary color scheme in red-violet, blue-violet, and yellow

The points of a square create a harmony of red-orange, yellow, blue-green, and violet

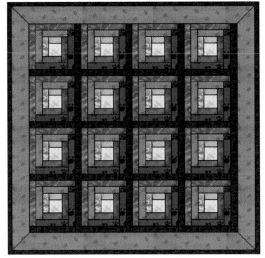

A rectangle creates a harmonious color scheme of orange, yellow, blue, and violet

PAGE 134

CHAPTER 5
Split Complementary Color Schemes

A split complementary color scheme is made from a color and the two neighbors of its complement

The same split complementary color scheme of red-violet, yellow and green

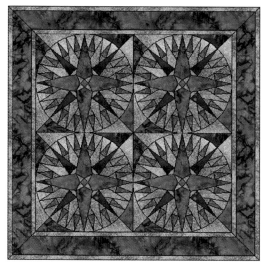

Split complements yellow-orange, blue, and violet

Split complements red, yellow-green, and blue-green

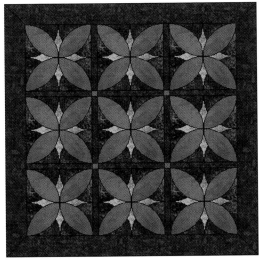

Not all earthtones are neutrals. Rust, for example, contains lots of red-orange. Thus it is usually too strong to remain neutral in a quilt.

Use neutrals in the background to calm down an overpowering color scheme

Scrap quilt with dark values in the points

Scrap quilt with dark values in the foreground

PAGE 158

CHAPTER 6
One-Color Quilts and Color Placement

One-color quilts can be dramatic — use
black to make pure colors sing

White makes a quiet background

The baskets in this quilt glow on a black
background

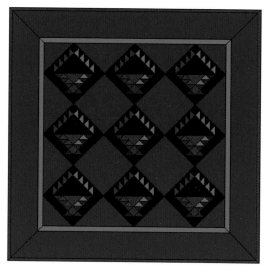

Red-violet overwhelms the baskets showing that
color, not placement, determines background

PAGES 164 & 172

Background and Foreground

Chapter 6

The Quiet of Neutrals & Earthtones

6

Color Theory

Neutrals and earthtones "tone down" (which literally means to add gray) and soften the contrast between vibrant colors. A quilt made mostly in neutrals (especially gray) or dull earthtones is quiet and restful.

True Neutrals

The true neutrals in color theory are black, white and gray. These are the achromatic colors we discussed in the Chroma lesson — the non-colors.

Quilters' Neutrals

To these true neutrals, quilters usually add pale beiges, creams or muslin, and related pale browns. Quilters use them as if they are white, non-colors, and even background. We can consider them neutrals too.

Earthtones

Earthtones are the browns, beiges and rusts of the earth. We're surrounded by earthtones in nature, where they act as a background for vivid blue skies, green grass and trees and vibrant hues of flowers.

Not all earthtones are neutrals. Rust, for example, contains lots of red-orange. Thus it is usually too strong to remain neutral in a quilt (although it's less dominant than the pure orange and red-orange it derives from).

Neutrals, Tones, and Earthtones in Quilts

Neutrals make good backgrounds. You want a background to stay in the background. Right? Then neutrals are naturals (forgive the pun!) as backgrounds. You can use them to calm down any overpowering color scheme.

Tones, especially dull earthtones, act to soften color contrast. Place them next to a color to reduce its brilliance. Or, try replacing the strong color with one of its tones or an earthtone. Both methods will mute a quilt, making it more subtle in color. A quilt made mostly in earthtones is quiet and restful.

Neutrals

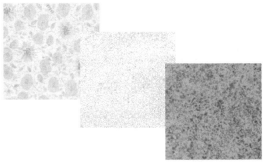

Quilters' Neutrals

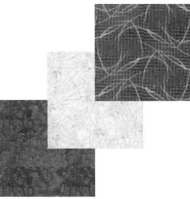

Earthtones

6

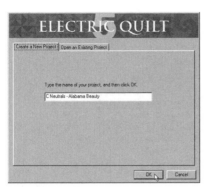

Steps 2-4

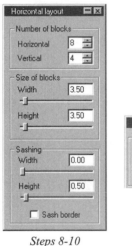

Steps 8-10

Step 12

Step 14

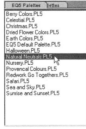

Step 15

Let's Play with Neutrals

1 Start EQ5.

2 Choose Create a New Project.

3 Type the name for your new project:
C Neutrals - Alabama Beauty.

4 Click OK.

5 Click Worktable — Work on Quilt.

Design the Quilt

Layout

6 Click Quilt — New Quilt — Horizontal.

7 Click the Layout tab along the bottom of
the screen.

8 Under Number of blocks, click the arrows to
read 8 Horizontal and 4 Vertical.

9 Under Size of blocks, drag the sliders to
read 3.50 Width and 3.50 Height.

10 Under Sashing, drag the sliders to read
width 0.00 and height 0.50. Be sure Sash
border is *not* checked. (Clicking will turn
this check on and off.)

Border

11 Click the Borders tab along the bottom of
the screen.

12 Click the Delete button so you have no
border.

13 Click the Layer 1 tab.

Collect the Fabrics

To color this quilt, you will choose fabrics from
the Palette Library.

14 Click Libraries — Palette Library — EQ5
Palettes.

15 Click Natural Neutrals, then the Load
button.

6

16 Choose "Delete all existing fabrics," then OK.

17 Click Libraries — Palette Library — EQ5 Palettes.

18 Click Earth Colors, then the Load button.

19 Choose "Don't delete any fabrics," then OK.

Organize the Fabrics in the Rows

20 Click the Paintbrush tool.

21 Scroll through the fabrics to see the fabrics you loaded.

22 Your quilt has four rows of eight squares each. If you do not have enough fabrics to fill a particular row, just repeat one or two.

23 Begin with Row 1 (the top row). Put only true neutrals (grays and other achromatic fabrics) in Row 1. Remember, you can always replace a fabric with a click if it doesn't belong.

24 Fill Row 2 with various Quilters' Neutrals (very light beiges).

25 Fill Row 3 with medium earthtones.

26 Fill Row 4 with dark earthtones.

27 Sit back and see if you need to rearrange any fabrics. Replace a fabric with a click if it doesn't belong in that row.

28 Click the Save in Sketchbook button.

You have now analyzed neutral and earthtone prints. Having them organized into four categories will help us when we design our quilt.

Earthtone Alabama Beauty Quilt
Layout

29 Click Quilt — New Quilt — Horizontal.

30 Click the Layout tab along the bottom of the screen.

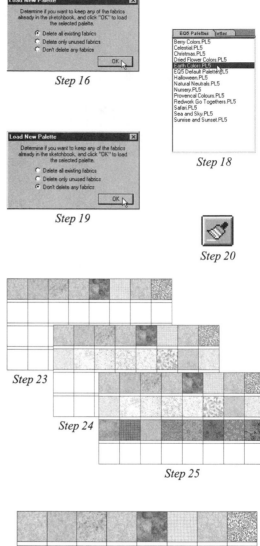

Step 16

Step 18

Step 19

Step 20

Step 23

Step 24

Step 25

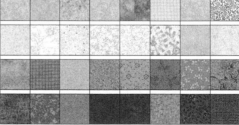

Step 26

Step 28

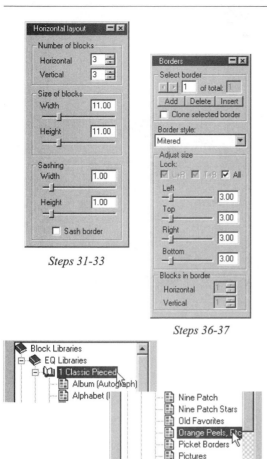

Steps 31-33

Steps 36-37

Step 39

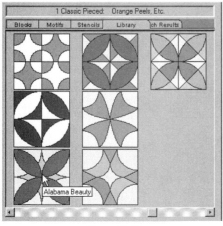

Steps 41-42

31 Under Number of blocks, click the arrows to read 3 Horizontal and 3 Vertical.

32 Under Size of blocks, drag the sliders to read 11.00 Width and 11.00 Height.

33 Under Sashing, drag the sliders to read 1.00 Width and 1.00 Height. Be sure Sash border is *not* checked. (Clicking here will turn this check on and off.)

Border

34 Click the Borders tab along the bottom of the screen.

35 Be sure there is a check next to All under Adjust size. (Clicking will turn this check on and off.)

36 You need one border. Click the Add button if you do not have a total of one border.

37 Drag one of the sliders to make it 3.00. All sides will adjust automatically.

38 Click the Layer 1 tab along the bottom of the screen.

Block

39 Click Libraries — Block Library — EQ Libraries — 1 Classic Pieced — Orange Peels, Etc.

40 Drag the horizontal scrollbar below the blocks to the right to see all the blocks in this book.

41 We want the Alabama Beauty block. Position your cursor over a block and the block name appears. If you still have the library set to view 9 blocks at a time, this block is in the bottom row, third column from the right.

42 Click on the Alabama Beauty block to select it. You'll see a frame around it to know it's the selected one.

6

43 Click Copy. The block disappears temporarily, indicating you've "copied" it into your Sketchbook.

44 Click Close.

45 Click the Set tool, then the Blocks tab. Click the Alabama Beauty block to select it.

46 Position your cursor over any block space in your empty quilt layout. Hold down your keyboard CTRL key and click. Your quilt is now filled with nine blocks.

Color the Quilts

47 Click the Paintbrush tool. The Fabric palette appears on the right.

48 You are going to make several earthtone quilts, using the fabrics you collected. For each quilt, follow these rules:

- Use a different color combination in every block

- The **four curved orange peels** should be the main design, so use strong colors (darks, rusts, golds) in these patches.

- The **four points behind the peels** should be colored in a bright strong color.

- The **background** is the space behind the peels and points. Use Quilters' Neutrals in these patches to make them recede.

- The **sashing** and border should enhance the colors in the center of the quilt. Try picking up the strongest or most colorful fabrics. Use a strong color in the cornerstones where the sashing strips overlap.

49 Save each quilt in the Sketchbook before starting a new color scheme.

Step 45

Step 46

Step 47

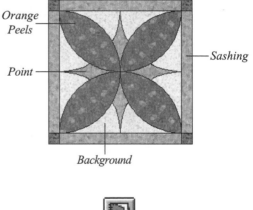

Orange Peels

Point

Sashing

Background

Step 49

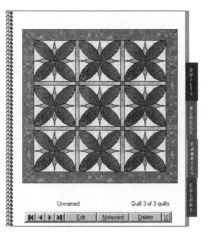
View your quilts in the Sketchbook

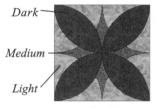
Dark — *Medium* — *Light*
Block 1

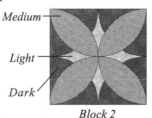
Medium — *Light* — *Dark*
Block 2

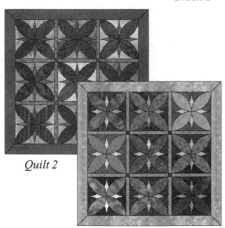
Quilt 2

Quilt 4

Study Your Quilts and Remember

- Click the View Sketchbook button, then the Quilts tab. Use the arrows to flip through a slide show of the different versions of the Alabama Beauty quilt.

- Because color is a first impression, flipping quickly through your quilts makes it very clear which colors stand out.

- What parts of the quilts stand out? What colors did you use in these pieces?

- See whether you achieved your goals as stated in Step 48. Analyze the colors to see why or why not.

- Are any of the quilts dull or uninteresting? Consider color as you decide why.

Suggestions for More Practice

- Try these 4 values and color schemes to see if you can control the design. Save each in your Sketchbook.

    Quilt 1 - CTRL + click to color all the blocks the same way. Make the petals dark, the points medium, and the background light, as in Block 1. Save in Sketchbook.

    Quilt 2 - Make a scrap quilt out of your current quilt. Use the same placement of values as in Quilt 1, but do not use the same fabric in more than one block. Save in Sketchbook.

    Quilt 3 - CTRL + click to color all the blocks the same way. Make the petals medium, the points light, and the background dark, as in Block 2. Save in Sketchbook.

    Quilt 4 - Make a scrap quilt out of your current quilt. Use the same placement of values as in Quilt 3, but do not use the same fabric in more than one block. Save in Sketchbook.

The Drama of One-Color Quilts

Color Theory

The background is just as important to a quilt as the foreground. When designing, think of the entire quilt as your design area. Don't allow yourself to think only in terms of individual blocks of different designs and color combinations. You should tie the blocks together and into the background. If you are aware that the background is important, you can blend the background and foreground together to avoid making quilts where the picture seems simply superimposed on the background. Using what we know about color can help you do this.

Positive and Negative Space

Artists and designers refer to the foreground as positive space and the background as negative space.

Positive space is the part of the quilt that contains the main design, the part that makes a statement and carries the theme of the quilt.

Negative space is the background of the quilt. You don't want to emphasize it or make it too busy, but you shouldn't ignore it either. Treat it gently and give it some life, otherwise it will become so dull that it goes unnoticed. Remember, negative space is there to support the foreground. Since it helps create the atmosphere and mood of the quilt, the background should work with the foreground. Tie them in together.

Finished quilt

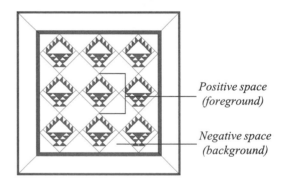

Positive space (foreground)

Negative space (background)

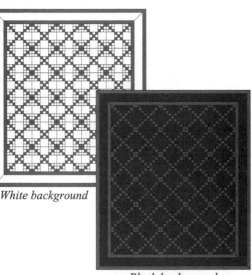

White background

Black background

Light Advances on Dark & Dark Advances on Light

Pure, light, or bright colors stand out or advance on a dark background. Dark, pure, or bright colors advance on a light background. This is because of contrast of value.

White and black are the most dramatic examples of dark and light backgrounds.

White makes a quiet background. It gives a light, clean, airy feeling, but the colors placed against it seem smaller and duller than they do on black.

Black makes pure colors sing. It makes a wonderful background for playing with color because it makes colors seem lighter and brighter than they really are.

The Drama of One-Color Quilts on Black or White Backgrounds

Simple one-color quilts are a mainstay of quiltmakers. They are dramatic in their simplicity, while the lack of multiple colors allows the graphic design to shine. In this lesson, we will play with one-color quilts, or quilts with one color on a black or white background.

1 Start EQ5.

2 Choose Create a New Project.

3 Type the name for your new project: C Drama Quilts - Amish Baskets.

4 Click OK.

5 Click Worktable — Work on Quilt.

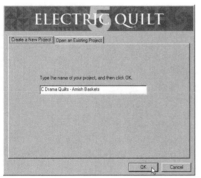

Steps 2-4

Step 5

6

Design the Quilt

Layout

6   Click Quilt — New Quilt — Horizontal.

7   Click the Layout tab along the bottom of the screen.

8   Under Number of blocks, click the arrows to read 5 Horizontal and 6 Vertical.

9   Under Size of blocks, drag the sliders to read 12.00 Width and 12.00 Height.

10   Under Sashing, drag both the sliders to read 0.00.

Borders

11   Click the Borders tab.

12   Click the Add button twice to make a total of 3 borders.

13   Be sure there is a check next to All under Adjust size. (Clicking will turn this check on and off.)

14   Click on the inner border. Drag one of the sliders to 1.50. All sides will adjust automatically.

15   Click on the middle border. Drag one of the sliders to read 4.00.

16   Click on the outer border. Drag one of the sliders to read 1.75.

17   Click the Layer 1 tab.

Blocks

18   You will collect two blocks for this lesson. Go to Libraries — Block Library — EQ Libraries — 2 Contemporary Pieced — Good Alternative Blocks.

19   Position your cursor over a block and the block name appears. You want to find the 9-Patch Chain block.

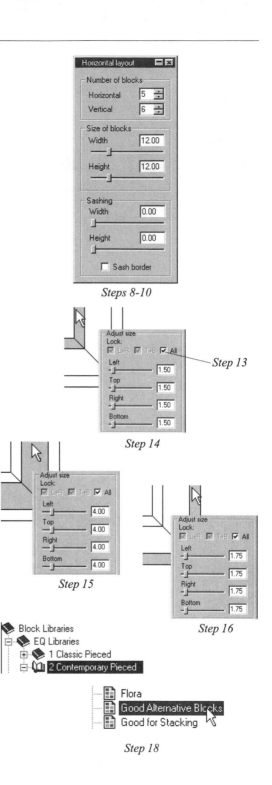

Steps 8-10

Step 13

Step 14

Step 15

Step 16

Step 18

6

Step 20

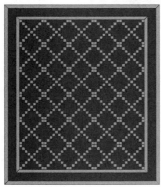

Step 22

Step 25   *Step 27*

Steps 28-31

20 Click on the 9-Patch Chain block to select it and click Copy. You'll notice that the block temporarily disappears, indicating you've "copied" it into your Sketchbook.

21 Still in 2 Contemporary Pieced, go to Baskets.

22 Find and click on the Amish Basket.

23 Click Copy to send a copy of the Amish Basket to your Sketchbook.

24 Click Close to return to the quilt worktable.

25 Click the Set tool.

26 Click the 9-Patch Chain block to select it, hold down the CTRL key on your keyboard and click in one square in the center of your quilt. All squares will fill with a fully colored 9-Patch Chain.

Color Quilt 1

27 Click the Spraycan tool (not the EQ4 spraycan) and then click on the Solids tab. You will use solids for this lesson.

28 Find **pure black** and click on it. The block currently is colored in red, white and beige.

29 CTRL + click to color beige and white sections of the center block and the middle border.

30 Click the Eyedropper tool and click on a **red** square in the 9-Patch Chain. (The Eyedropper will pick up the red and automatically switch you back to the Spraycan tool so you can color again.)

6

31 CTRL + click to color the inner and outer borders red, while leaving the middle border black.

32 Save this quilt in the Sketchbook.

Step 32

Step 33

33 Now that we have the borders colored individually we can use the Swap tool. Click the Swap tool and click on **white** in the Palette.

34 Click the black background to change it to white.

35 Save this quilt in the Sketchbook.

36 Click the View Sketchbook button, then the Quilts tab. Look at the two quilts. Pure red on black or white is always a successful color scheme.

Step 36

Step 35

37 Close the Sketchbook by clicking on the X in the bottom-right corner.

38 Still using the Swap tool, change the red to **pure blue**. Save this quilt in the Sketchbook.

39 Click on **black** in the palette. Use the Swap tool to change all the white patches to black.

40 Save the quilt in the Sketchbook.

41 Optional: Color two more versions of this quilt, using any pure colors you want. I recommend **yellow** and **blue-green**. Make a white background and a black background for any you choose.

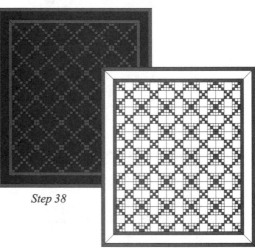

Step 38

Step 39

Let's Play with another Classic One-Color Quilt Design

Layout

42 Click Quilt — New Quilt — On-point.

43 Click the Layout tab along the bottom of the screen.

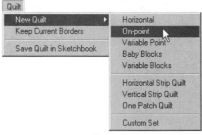

Step 42

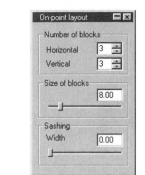

Steps 44-46

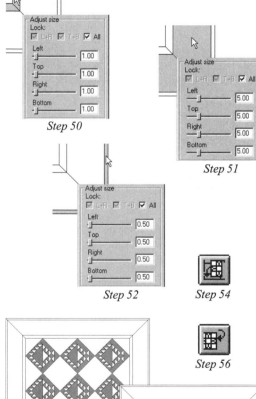

Step 50

Step 51

Step 52

Step 54

Step 56

Step 55

Step 57

44 Under Number of blocks, click the arrows to read 3 Horizontal and 3 Vertical.

45 Under Size of blocks, drag the sliders to read 8.00 Width.

46 Under Sashing, drag the slider to read 0.00.

Border

47 Click the Borders tab.

48 Click the Add button twice to make a total of 3 borders.

49 Be sure there is a check next to All under Adjust Size. (Clicking will turn this check on and off.)

50 Click on the inner border. Drag one of the sliders to 1.00. All sides will adjust automatically.

51 Click on the middle border. Drag one of the sliders to read 5.00.

52 Click on the outer border. Drag one of the sliders to read 0.50.

Block

53 Click the Layer 1 tab.

54 Click the Set tool.

55 Click on the Amish Basket block. Before putting it into the quilt, look at the quilt layout. It consists of five rows. Rows 1, 3 and 5 contain three full blocks while Rows 2 and 4 contain two full blocks. CTRL + click on the center block in row 3 to insert the Amish Basket into all the squares in Rows 1, 3 and 5. Leave the squares in Rows 2 and 4 empty.

56 Click the Rotate tool.

57 CTRL + click on the Amish Basket in your quilt to rotate all the blocks once.

6

6

Color the Quilt

58 Click the Spraycan tool and click on the Solids tab.

59 Find **pure blue** and click on it. Look at the coloration of the blocks as they were imported. The basket is white on a rust background. You need to color all the white basket patches in the pure blue. Use CTRL + click to change all patches in all blocks at once.

60 Now color the inner and outer borders in the same blue, just as you did in the last quilt.

61 Find and click on **pure black** in the palette.

62 Use CTRL + click to color all of the rest of the quilt and the middle border black.

63 Save this quilt in the Sketchbook.

Look at the blue on black basket quilt. The pure blue glows on the black background. This color scheme of one pure solid on a solid black background is a typical Amish formula, and it is always dramatic! Black always makes color sing, especially pure colors.

64 Click the Swap tool and click on **white**. Change the black background to white and save the quilt in the Sketchbook.

65 Click on **pure red** in the palette. Change the blue baskets to red and save the quilt in the Sketchbook.

66 Click on **black** in the palette and change the white background to black. Save this quilt in the Sketchbook.

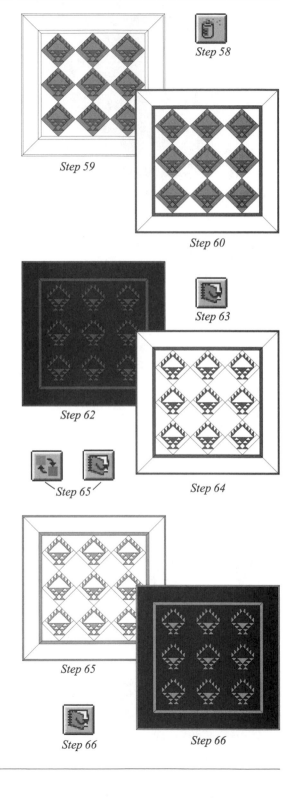

Step 58

Step 59

Step 60

Step 63

Step 62

Step 65

Step 64

Step 65

Step 66

Step 66

Study your One-Color Quilts

6

67 Color and save two more versions of this quilt, using any pure colors you want. Do a white background and a black background for each. I recommend two popular Amish colors for the baskets: red-violet and violet. Choose a medium-value violet if the dark one doesn't show up well.

Study your One-Color Quilts

- Click the View Sketchbook button, then the Quilts tab. Use the arrows to flip through a slide show of all the one-color quilts.

- Notice how different the pure colors look on white and on black.

- Notice how the colored borders complete the design and act as frames to hold the quilt together.

Remember

- A quilt of one pure color on white or black will always be dramatic.

- A white background softens colors while a black background enhances them.

- Crisp, graphic quilt designs look elegant in a one-color on black or white color scheme.

Color, Not Placement, Determines Background

Color Theory

6

Color is the first thing people see when they look at a quilt. Depending on where you put your colors, you can emphasize or de-emphasize different parts of your quilt. Sometimes color can change the dynamics of background and foreground. Let's play with the Amish Baskets quilt to see how this works.

Use the Existing Quilt

1   Start EQ5.

2   Choose Open an Existing Project.

3   Click on the name of the project in the Most Recently Used Projects or Existing Projects list: C Drama Quilts - Amish Baskets.

4   Click OK.

5   The Sketchbook will appear. Click the Quilts tab.

6   Use the arrows to scroll to find one of the Amish Baskets quilts with a white background.

7   Click the Edit button to place it on the quilt worktable.

Color the Quilt

You will use solids for this lesson. You are going to color all spaces in the block in as pleasing a combination of the pure or close-to-pure versions of these Amish colors as you can get: red-violet, violet, blue-violet, blue and blue-green.

8   Click the Paintbrush tool. Click the Solids tab on the palette.

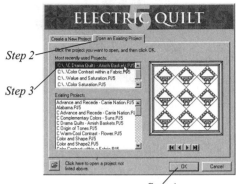

Step 2

Step 3

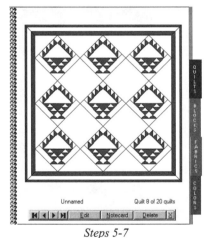

Step 4

Steps 5-7

Step 8

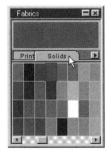

Step 8

6

Steps 10-14

Step 15

Step 16

Steps 16-17

Step 18

Step 19

9 Find and click on **blue-violet** in the palette.

10 Hold down the CTRL key on your keyboard and click (CTRL + click) to color the triangles on the left side of the handle, as well as the two inner (white) triangles on the left side of the basket. (Patches labeled "10" in the image to the left.) All baskets should color at the same time.

11 Find and click on **blue-green** in the palette. CTRL + click to color the same sections of the block except on the right side this time. (Patches labeled "11".)

12 Find and click on **pure blue**. CTRL + click to color the center basket triangle and the bottom square.

13 Find and click on **pure red-violet**. CTRL + click to color the outer-left side of the basket and the bottom-right leg of the basket.

14 Find and click on **violet**. CTRL + click to color the outer-right side of the basket and the bottom-left leg of the basket.

15 Click the Save in Sketchbook button.

16 Click the Spraycan tool (not the EQ4 Spraycan tool) and click on **black** in the palette. CTRL + click in the large triangular space inside the basket handle. The "background" of the basket will color black.

17 Color the inner and outer borders in one or two of the colors in the blocks. Leave the middle border white.

18 Save this white background quilt in the Sketchbook.

19 Click on **black** in the palette. CTRL + click on a background square in the quilt, in other words, a white on-point square, to change all the white background to black.

6

For all of the next changes, keep the same block coloration, make the changes, and save the quilt in the Sketchbook.

20 Change the middle border to **black** and Save in Sketchbook.

21 Change all three borders to three different colors from the blocks and Save in Sketchbook.

22 Change the on-point background squares to a **pure blue-green** and Save in Sketchbook.

23 Change the middle border to a **pure blue-green** and Save in Sketchbook.

24 Change the on-point background squares and middle border to **pure yellow** and Save in Sketchbook.

25 Change the on-point background squares and middle border to **bright red-violet** (R:255 G:O B:102) and Save in Sketchbook.

Study your Amish Baskets Quilts

• Click the View Sketchbook button and then the Quilts tab. Use the arrows to flip through a slide show of all the Amish Baskets quilts.

• As you stop on each quilt, notice which color you see first. Analyze why.

• Study each quilt to see whether the blocks stand out against the background or become lost in it. Even though your block is made of strong pure colors, the color of the background changes how strong they appear. The yellow and red-violet backgrounds probably overwhelm the baskets.

Remember

• Color, not placement, determines what part of a quilt we see at first glance. This is a concept well worth understanding.

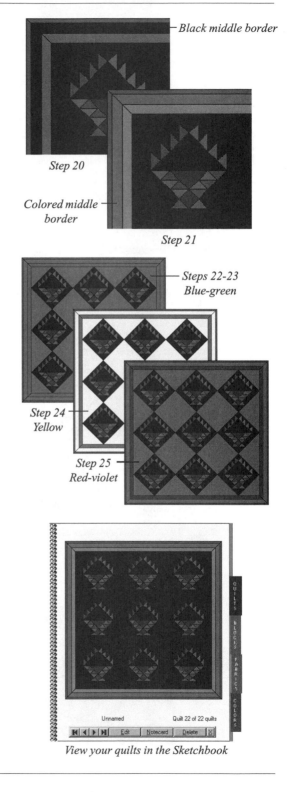

— *Black middle border*

Step 20

Colored middle border —

Step 21

— *Steps 22-23 Blue-green*

Step 24 Yellow

Step 25 Red-violet

View your quilts in the Sketchbook

Perspective and Dimension

Chapter 7

Perspective Through Light and Shadow

Let's play with light and shadow in an Attic Window block.

1 Start EQ5.

2 Choose Create a New Project.

3 Type the name for your new project: C Light & Shadow - Attic Window.

4 Click OK.

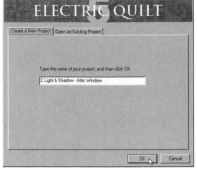

7

5 Click Worktable — Work on Quilt.

Design the Quilt

Layout

6 Click Quilt — New Quilt — Horizontal.

7 Click the Layout tab.

8 Under Number of blocks, click the arrows to read 3 Horizontal and 4 Vertical.

9 Under Size of blocks, drag the sliders to read 8.00 width and 8.00 height.

10 Under Sashing, drag both the sliders to read 0.00.

Borders

11 Click the Borders tab.

12 Click the Add button once to make a total of 2 borders.

13 Click on the inner border.

14 Be sure there is a check next to All under Adjust size. (Clicking will turn this check on and off.)

15 Drag the left slider to 1.00. All sides will adjust together automatically.

16 Click on the outer border.

17 Drag the left slider to 2.25. All sides will adjust together automatically.

18 Click the Layer 1 tab.

Steps 2-4

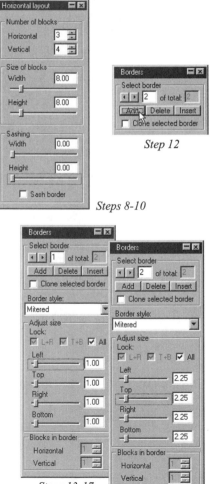

Step 12

Steps 8-10

Steps 13-17

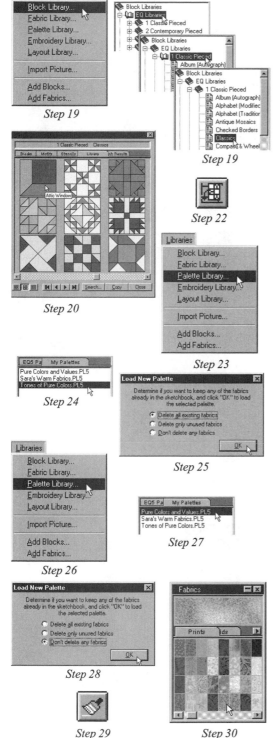

Step 19

Step 19

Step 22

Step 20

Step 23

Step 24

Step 25

Step 26

Step 27

Step 28

Step 29

Step 30

Block

19 Click Libraries — Block Library — EQ Libraries — 1 Classic Pieced — Classics.

20 Find and click on the Attic Window block.

21 Click the Copy button, then Close.

22 Click the Set tool, then the Blocks tab. Click the Attic Window block to select it. CTRL + click in the quilt. All blocks are now filled with the Attic Window.

Collect the Fabrics

23 Click Libraries — Palette Library — My Palettes tab.

24 Click your Tones of Pure Colors palette, and click Load.

25 Choose "Delete all existing fabrics," then click OK.

26 Click Libraries — Palette Library — My Palettes tab.

27 Click your Pure Colors and Values palettes, and click Load.

28 Choose "Don't delete any fabrics," and click OK.

Quilt 1: Attic Window in Grays

See how the quilt looks like a twelve-pane window with a frame around it? We will treat it as a window, pretending that light is shining fully on the lower windowsill and each block's left side is in deep shadow.

29 Click the Paintbrush tool, then the Prints tab in the palette.

30 Choose a **sky-like blue or cloud print**. Hold down your keyboard CTRL key and click on the center square in a block on your quilt. All will fill with the same fabric.

31 Choose a **medium gray** print (it can have a cast of a color) and CTRL + click to put it into the bottom sill in all blocks.

7

32 Choose a **deeper gray** and CTRL + click to put it into the left sill in all blocks.

33 The illusion should look like light sky in the window, with light falling on the bottom sill and shadow on the left sill. Change fabrics until you find the best trio of colors.

34 Color the inner border in a different **darker gray or toned color** and the outer border in a **dark gray or black**.

35 Save this quilt in the Sketchbook.

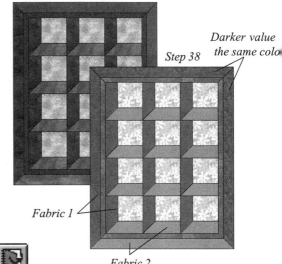

Step 35

Step 34

Quilt 2: An Attic Window in Values of Different Color Schemes

36 Repeat Steps 29-35, keeping the placement of sky, light and shadows, but making them more colorful. Use light, medium, and dark values of any color in a variety of prints to create a monochromatic color scheme.

37 Save this quilt in the Sketchbook.

38 Let's continue the illusion into the *outer border*. Color the left side in the same print as the left windowsill. Color the bottom side in the same print as the bottom sill. Make the top and right sides of the outer border a darker value of the same color.

39 Save this quilt in the Sketchbook.

Darker value the same color

Step 38

Fabric 1

Fabric 2

Step 39

Quilt 3: An Attic Window Scrap Quilt

An Attic Window quilt makes a wonderful scrap quilt. Since value controls the illusion of light and shadow, you can use many fabrics. Place dark fabrics on the left sill, medium fabrics in the bottom sill, and light in the center. Use light floral prints in the center since it is a large space.

40 Repeat Steps 29-35, keeping the placement of sky, light and shadows the same, but changing the color scheme for each block.

41 Color the left and bottom sides in the same color as one of the left and bottom sills, thus continuing the illusion of light shining in.

42 Save this scrap quilt in the Sketchbook.

Step 42

Steps 40-42

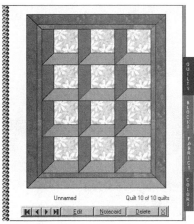

View your Sketchbook

Remove the borders

Set up the quilt

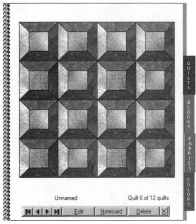

*Practice your light and shadow technique
with the Lattice Square block*

Study the Attic Window Quilts and Remember

- To see the quilts you made, click the View Sketchbook button and then the Quilts tab. Use the arrows to flip through your quilts from beginning to end.

- Look for how well the illusion of light and shadow works in each quilt.

- Do any colors stand out too much or distort the illusion? These colors can be changed.

- Does continuing the illusion in the borders enhance the quilt designs?

- You have mixed value and color in choosing the dark and medium fabrics. Are there colors that appear stronger than you thought they would? If yes, why?

- Remember that you can create the illusion of light and shadow through placement of color and value.

Suggestions for More Light and Shadow Practice

- Click Libraries — Block Library — EQ Libraries — 1 Classic Pieced — Four Patch. Copy the Lattice Square block to your project.

Start a new 2x2 horizontal quilt with no sashing and no borders.

Use five values to color the blocks with light shining in from the right and the darkest value at the bottom. Save any quilts you like in your Sketchbook.

7

Dimension Through Light and Shadow

The Thousand Pyramids quilt is often a scrap quilt. Rarely do quilters use it to create a light and shadow effect. But why can't a scrap quilt have a controlled illusion, too? It is easy and fun to give this simple diamond and triangle quilt depth.

All you have to do is to control the placement of dark versus light values, and dull versus saturated colors.

Let's Play with Light and Shadow in a Thousand Pyramids Quilt

1 Start EQ5.

2 Choose Create a New Project.

3 Type the name for your new project: C Light & Shadow - 1000 Pyramids.

4 Click OK.

5 Click Worktable — Work on Quilt.

Design the Quilt

Layout

6 Click Quilt — New Quilt — One Patch Quilt. You will see a hexagon layout, but don't worry.

7 Click the Layout tab along the bottom of the screen.

8 Under Patch style, click the dropdown arrow and scroll down to click on Thousand Pyramids.

9 Under Number of Units, click the arrows to read 6 Horizontal and 6 Vertical.

10 Under Size of Units, drag the sliders to read 7.00 Width and 7.00 Height.

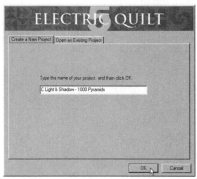

Steps 2-4

Step 6

Step 7

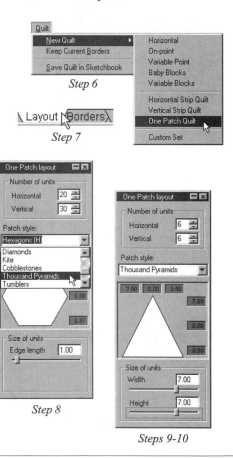

Step 8

Steps 9-10

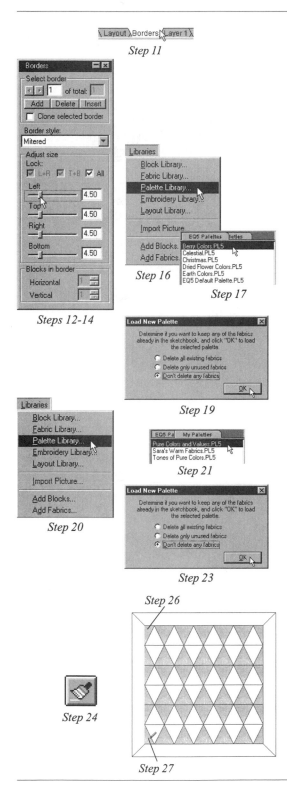

Step 11

Steps 12-14

Step 16

Step 17

Step 19

Step 20

Step 21

Step 23

Step 24

Step 26

Step 27

Borders

11 Click the Borders tab.

12 You want one border. Click the Add button if you do not have one already.

13 Be sure there is a check next to All under Adjust Size. (Clicking will turn this check on and off.)

14 Drag the left slider to read 4.50. All sides will adjust automatically.

15 Click the Layer 1 tab.

Collect the Fabrics for the Quilt

16 Click Libraries — Palette Library — EQ5 Palettes tab.

17 Click the Berry Colors palette, then Load.

18 Choose "Don't delete any fabrics," and click OK.

19 Repeat Steps 16-18 for the Celestial palette.

20 Click Libraries — Palette Library — My Palettes tab.

21 Click on the Pure Colors and Values palette.

22 Click the Load button.

23 Choose "Don't delete any fabrics," and click OK.

Color the Quilt

24 Click the Paintbrush tool.

25 Scroll through the Fabrics palette, find and click on a **light gray-blue**. This will be the background fabric.

26 CTRL + click on the corner half-triangle in the upper-left corner of the quilt. All the pieces in that row will turn blue.

27 CTRL + click on the corner half-triangle in the bottom-left corner of the quilt. This will color the rest of background blue.

7

Look at the quilt. You now have diamonds and the border. Let's work on the diamonds.

28 Color the bottom-halves of the diamonds (the bottom triangles) in a variety of **dark, jewel-like prints**. Use vivid prints in both warm and cool. You can repeat fabrics but probably won't have to.

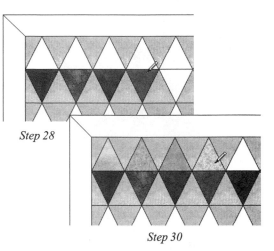

Step 28

29 After filling all of the bottom triangles, take a moment to look at the prints. Change some around and make sure warm and cool are spread out and balanced.

30 Now color the top-halves of the diamonds (the top triangles) with **light or medium values**. Make sure the values are either of the color below it or of an analogous color. Use pretty prints to add interest.

Step 30

31 Save this quilt in the Sketchbook.

Color Different Borders and Change the Background

Step 31

32 Still using the Paintbrush tool, make several versions of the quilt:
- Change to different border and background prints.
- Save each one in the Sketchbook.
- For the borders, repeat vivid darks from the lower triangles.
- For the background, try light values in a variety of cool and warm colors.
- While coloring, use the CTRL key on your keyboard to make your changes more quickly.

Tip

Be careful as you click colors into the background that you don't erase your diamonds. If you catch the mistake immediately, choose Edit — Undo from the top menu bar. Otherwise if you accidentally erase the diamonds at any time, open the Sketchbook, find the last quilt you were working on, and click the Edit button. It will now be on your quilt worktable.

Step 32

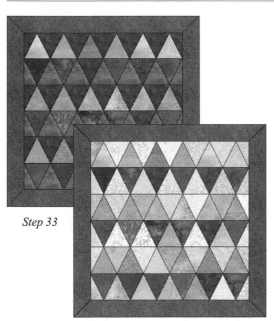

Step 33

Step 34

Step 35

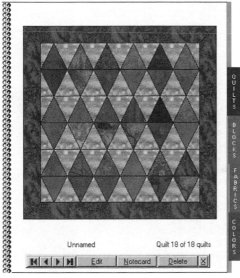

View your quilts in the Sketchbook

Add Interest to the Background

33 Try making the upper rows of the background a **slightly different value** of the bottom row's color. CTRL + click on the corner half-triangle in the upper-left corner of the quilt to do this.

34 Try making every background piece a different fabric, but keep all background patches **light values**.

35 Save all versions of the quilt in the Sketchbook.

Change the Diamonds

All of the diamonds are dark on the bottom and light on the top. Let's change them so they are completely dark.

36 Leave the bottom fabrics the same, but change the top fabrics to **any color that goes well with the dark fabric** — warm or cool, analogous is good. Just keep them dark.

37 Try different light backgrounds and different borders.

38 Save all or just the ones you like in the Sketchbook.

Study Your Quilts

• Click the View Sketchbook button and then the Quilts tab. Use the arrows to flip through and admire the quilts you made.

• Look at the quilts to see which quilts best achieve the illusion of light and shadow.

• Notice how different sky or background fabrics change the design.

• See if you can use what you know about color to figure out why for both.

7

Remember

- You can use value to create the illusion of light and shadow.

- The color and value of a fabric is more important than the print in controlling what the viewer sees.

Suggestions for More Practice with Light and Shadow

- Go to Libraries — Block Library — EQ Libraries — 1 Classic Pieced — Old Favorites. Copy the Chinese Lanterns block to your project. Start a new 5 x 5 horizontal quilt. Make the blocks 5.50 x 5.50 and the sashing 1.00 x 1.00. Set the borders to:

    Border 1 — 1.00, Corner Blocks

    Border 2 — 4.25, Mitered

    Border 3 — 1.00, Mitered

- Color the Lanterns in the same manner as you did for the thousand pyramids, maintaining the light prints on top and dark prints on bottom coloring scheme. Use a variety of prints or analogous colors. Just be sure to keep the top prints of the same value, and the bottom prints of the same value.

- Color the background of the jewels and border 2 the same with a background sky fabric.

- Color the sashing, and borders 1 and 3 the same with a dark fabric used in one of the jewels.

- Save this quilt in the Sketchbook.

- Try using ALT + click to color every other lantern in cool colors, then use ALT + click to color the remaining lanterns in warm colors.

- Save any quilts you like in the Sketchbook.

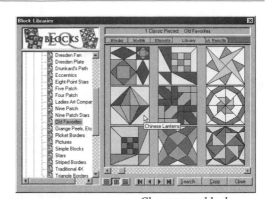

Choose your block

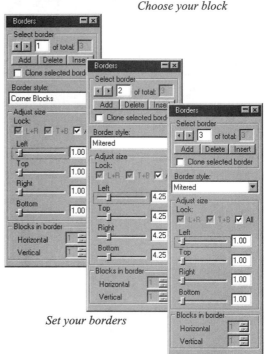

Set your borders

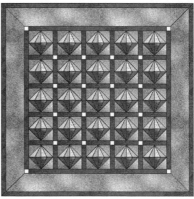

Color the practice Lantern quilt

Special Effects and Optical Illusions

Chapter 8

Understanding Transparency Using Solids

Color Theory

Transparency is a delightful illusion that can be created with color. It is one of the few color concepts that requires a formula to succeed. But it is worth learning about and experimenting with because it can add great beauty and richness to your quilts.

There are three basic formulas for creating the effect of transparency:

Use **three analogous colors** from the color wheel. Use the two outer analogous colors as the colors that will overlap. Use the middle color where they overlap. To be successful, use three colors that have similar values and level of saturation (grayness). You usually don't mix pure colors and tones in this formula.

Use **three values of one color**. To create the illusion that dark and light are overlapping, use the middle value where the colors cross. This illusion works well with grayed tones of colors.

Use **any two colors and a darker version of one of those two colors**. Put the darker value in the overlapping area. If you are combining a warm and a cool color, try using a dark value of the warm color. This seems to help the illusion, probably because warm colors are stronger and would stand out more in real life.

The background, while not essential to the illusion of transparency, can enhance it.

Let's Play with Transparency

1   Start EQ5.

2   Choose Create a New Project.

3   Type the name for your new project:
    C Transparency - Solid Plaids.

4   Click OK.

5   Click Worktable — Work on Quilt.

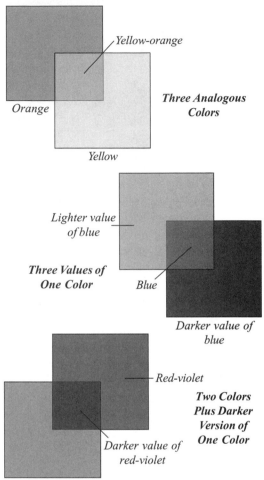

Yellow-orange

Orange

Yellow

Three Analogous Colors

Lighter value of blue

Blue

Three Values of One Color

Darker value of blue

Red-violet

Darker value of red-violet

Blue-green

Two Colors Plus Darker Version of One Color

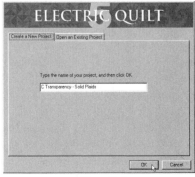

Steps 2-4

8

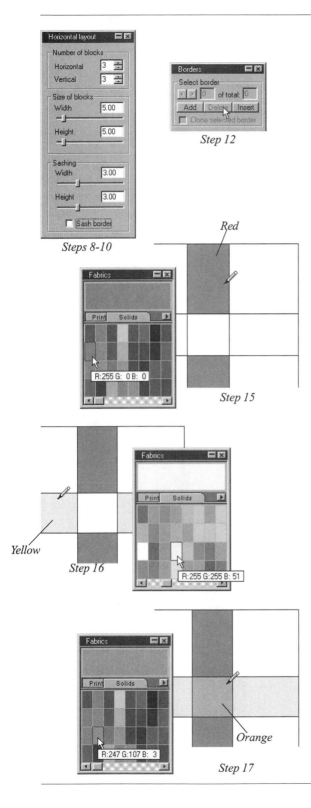

Steps 8-10

Step 12

Red

Step 15

Yellow

Step 16

Orange

Step 17

Design the Quilt
Layout

6 Click Quilt — New Quilt — Horizontal.

7 Click the Layout tab along the bottom of the screen.

8 Under Number of blocks, click the arrows to read 3 Horizontal and 3 Vertical.

9 Under Size of blocks, drag the sliders to read 5.00 Width and 5.00 Height.

10 Under Sashing, drag both the sliders to read 3.00. Be sure Sash border is *not* checked. (Clicking here will turn this check on and off.)

Borders

11 Click the Borders tab along the bottom of the screen.

12 Click the Delete button to eliminate all borders.

13 Click the Layer 1 tab along the bottom of the screen.

Method 1: *Three Analogous Colors*
Quilt 1: Using Yellow and Red Stripes

Notice how your quilt is made up of large squares, horizontal and vertical stripes (the sashes), and small squares where the stripes cross. We will treat it as a plaid.

14 Click the Paintbrush tool. Click on the Solids tab.

15 Choose a **bright red** and CTRL + click to put red into the two vertical stripes.

16 Choose a **bright yellow** and CTRL + click to put yellow into the two horizontal stripes.

17 Choose a **bright orange** and CTRL + click to color the squares where the red and yellow stripes cross.

8

18 Lean back and study the illusion. You can change colors until you find the best trio of colors for your transparency.

19 Click Save in Sketchbook.

20 Find a **dark orange** and CTRL + click to color the squares where the red and yellow cross.

21 Click Save in Sketchbook.

22 Find a **pastel orange** and CTRL + click to color the squares where the red and yellow cross.

23 Click Save in Sketchbook.

24 Click on your bright orange, used in Step 17. Right-click on it and choose Add Tones.

25 Click the Add to Sketchbook button.

26 Scroll to the right to find the ten new tones you added to the right end of the palette.

27 Find a **middle orange tone** and CTRL + click to color the squares where the red and yellow cross.

28 Click Save in Sketchbook.

You just changed the orange in value and saturation. Notice how the illusion of transparency changes and may become less successful as you recolor the area where red and yellow overlap.

Quilt 1: Color the Background

29 Find your **bright orange** again and CTRL + click to color the squares where the red and yellow cross.

30 CTRL + click to color the large background squares in the **lightest yellow or gold** you can find.

31 Click Save in Sketchbook.

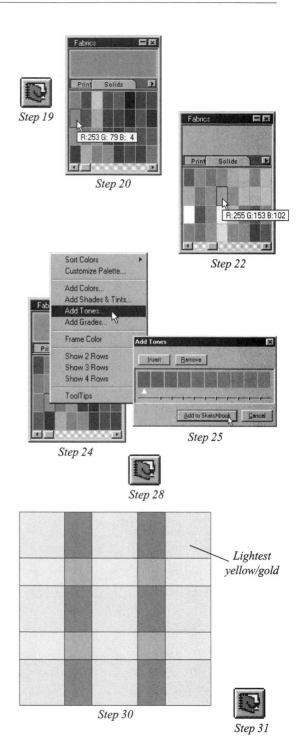

Step 19

Step 20

Step 22

Step 24

Step 25

Step 28

Lightest yellow/gold

Step 30

Step 31

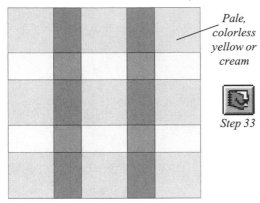

Pale, colorless yellow or cream

Step 32

Step 33

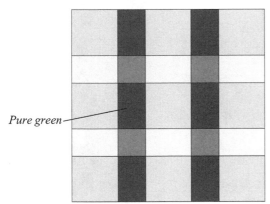

Pure green

Step 35

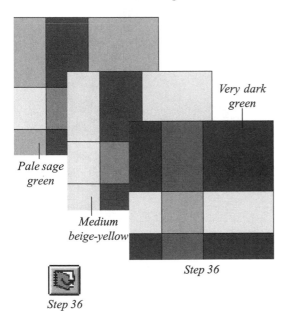

Very dark green

Pale sage green

Medium beige-yellow

Step 36

Step 36

32 Replace the light yellow or gold with any **pale, colorless yellow or cream**.

33 Click Save in Sketchbook.

34 The background color, while not essential to the illusion, often enhances it. Try a very dark and then a very light value of one of the colors to see how different the plaid looks against these new backgrounds. Save each in your Sketchbook.

Notice when you change the background how the entire block changes subtly.

Real plaids are, of course, woven stripes of colors that overlap, and the color changes slightly in this overlapping area. So a plaid block makes the perfect venue for experimenting with transparency.

This block is quick to color, so make *many* samples and save them in your Sketchbook for later study.

8

⚲ Tip

If at any time you want to start fresh with a plain quilt, just CTRL + click solid white all over your quilt where you see color.

Quilt 2: Using Yellow, Green and Yellow-Green

35 CTRL + click and change the two vertical stripes to a **pure green**. Now you have green and yellow stripes overlapping, and where they do, you should use the analogous color between them: **Yellow-green**. In the basic EQ palette, there are two yellow-greens. Try CTRL + clicking in each of them and use the one that works best.

36 Change the background three times: to a **pale sage green**, a **medium beige-yellow**, and a **very dark green**. Don't forget to save each in the Sketchbook.

Try Other Analogous Colors Combinations

37 Do several more examples using analogous colors to create the illusion of transparency. Try any three colors on the color wheel and save only successful quilts in the Sketchbook.

Method 2: Quilts Designed Around
Three Values of a Color

Now we will use the three-value formula for creating transparency to make the dark and light colors seem to overlap. To do this, we'll use the middle value where the colors cross. Remember, this illusion works well with grayed tones of colors.

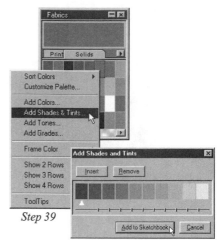

Step 39

Step 39

38 CTRL + click **white** everywhere in your quilt to start over.

39 Click on any pure color you like. Right-click on it and choose Add Shades & Tints. Click Add to Sketchbook.

40 Scroll to the right on the palette to find the ten values you added.

Look at the ten solids. Notice that the lightest value is almost white and the darkest is very dark. For your transparency play, I suggest you play with values 3, 5 and 7 (consider the lightest as #1). You can always replace these with 4 and/or 6 if the illusion doesn't seem clear enough.

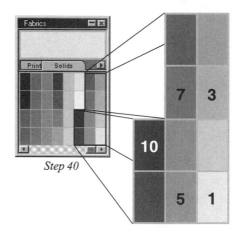

Step 40

41 Click on **Value 3** and CTRL + click to put it into the two horizontal stripes.

42 Click on **Value 5** and CTRL + click to color the cross squares.

43 Click on **Value 7** and CTRL + click to put it into the two vertical stripes.

44 Lean back and study the illusion. Change any of the values until you find the best trio of colors.

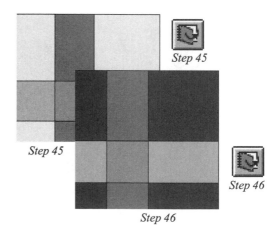

Step 45

Step 45

Step 46

Step 46

45 Color the background in the **lightest value** (Value 1) and click Save in Sketchbook.

46 Color the background in the **darkest value** (Value 10) and click Save in Sketchbook.

47 Repeat Steps 38-46 for several more Three-Value Quilts.

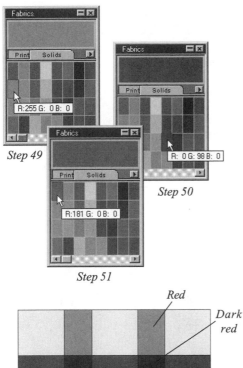

Step 49

Step 50

Step 51

Method 3: *Two Contrasting Colors*
Complementary Colors and One Value
In this quilt we'll use complements. The colors are total opposites, but make a harmonious color scheme. Let's begin with pure red and green.

48 CTRL + click **white** everywhere in your quilt to start over.

49 Choose a **pure red** and CTRL + click to put red into the two vertical stripes.

50 Choose a **pure green** and CTRL + click to put green into the two horizontal stripes.

51 Choose a **dark red** and CTRL + click to color the squares where the red and green stripes cross.

Lean back and study the illusion. You can change color in each piece until you find the best trio of colors. Try changing the dark red first.

52 If you don't think you have enough values of your complements, do the following: Right-click on either red or green, choose Add Shades & Tints, and click Add to Sketchbook.

53 Color the background in a **very light value** of either color.

54 Repeat Steps 48-54, using pairs of other complementary colors. Save successful quilts in the Sketchbook.

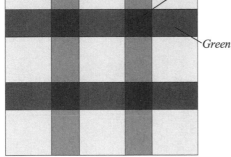

Red

Dark red

Green

Step 53

Step 54

8

Method 3: *Two Colors*
Adding Grades to Mix Any Two Colors

When you think of a plaid, you have two colors; and where they cross they seem to mix. So why can't we mix the colors in EQ? Let's try it. Don't forget to CTRL + click **white** everywhere to start with a blank quilt.

55 Choose a **pure red** and CTRL + click to put red into the two vertical stripes.

56 Right-click on **red** and choose Add Grades. You'll see a new box appear with *two colors* at the top and a small version of *all your colors* at the bottom. A large red swatch will be on one side at the top and yellow on the other.

57 Click Add to Sketchbook.

58 Scroll to the right end of the palette. You now have ten new colors starting at red and mixing into yellow.

59 CTRL + click this **last yellow** into the two horizontal stripes.

60 Use a **middle grade** (Grade 5 or 6) and CTRL + click it into the cross squares.

61 Click Save in Sketchbook.

62 Replace the cross square color using CTRL + click with a **grade that is closer to red**. Click Save in Sketchbook.

63 Replace this color using CTRL + click with a **grade that is closer to yellow** and *watch what happens to the illusion.*

64 Click Save in Sketchbook.

65 Notice that when you choose a grade closer to one color than the other, it may even seem like that color is on top. Let's try it again, just to be sure. CTRL + click in a grade closer to red and it looks like red is on top of yellow. CTRL + click in a grade closer to yellow and it looks like yellow is on top of red.

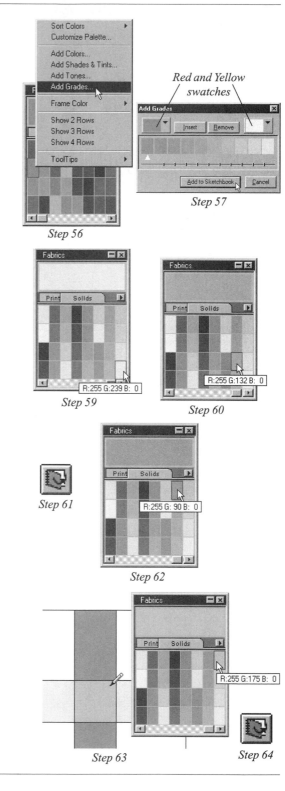

Red and Yellow swatches

Step 57

Step 56

Step 59

Step 60

Step 61

Step 62

Step 63

Step 64

8

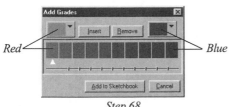

Steps 67-68

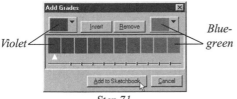

Red ← ← → Blue

Step 68

Violet ← ← → Blue-green

Step 71

What if we don't want to use yellow? You can choose your colors from the dropdown menus.

66 Right-click on **red** again and choose Add Grades. The same box will appear with red on one side and yellow on the other.

67 Click on the large yellow swatch at the top and a dropdown of all your color choices will appear. You can mix red with any of the other colors in your palette.

68 Click on a **pure blue** in this dropdown of color choices. You should now see red mixed with blue.

Tip

"Help! My dropdown is too close to the right side of my screen. I can't see all my colors or the scrollbar!"

All you need to do is click on any color to close the dropdown; it doesn't matter which one. (No colors will be added yet.) Click to move the blue title bar of the Add Grades box to the left and up away from the edge of your screen. Click the dropdown menu again and now you should see all your colors and the complete scrollbar.

8

69 What if I don't want red? Click on the large red swatch and choose a different color from the dropdown of choices.

70 What if I don't want blue? Click on the large blue swatch and choose a different color from the dropdown of choices.

71 Choose two colors you want to mix and when you like what you see, click the Add to Sketchbook button.

72 Scroll to the right end of the palette to see these ten added grades.

73 CTRL + click Grade 1 into the horizontal stripes.

74 CTRL + click Grade 10 into the vertical stripes.

75 CTRL + click any middle grade into the cross squares.

Steps 73-75

76 Change the color of the cross squares as needed to help the illusion.

77 Click Save in Sketchbook when you're finished.

Step 77

Study the Transparency Quilts and Remember

- To see the quilts you made, click View Sketchbook, then the Quilts tab. Use the arrows to flip through the plaids from beginning to end.

- Look for how well the illusion of transparency works in each plaid. Ask yourself what makes some more successful than others.

- Identify the formula you used in each plaid.

- Remember the three formulas for your future enjoyment.

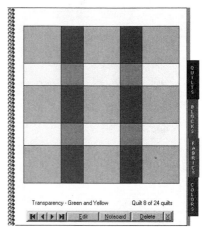

View your plaids in the Sketchbook

8

8

Adding Transparency to Blocks Using Prints

Color Theory

This second lesson in transparency is fun and simple. In the previous lesson you learned the three formulas for creating transparency. Let's experiment with this exciting illusion.

Let's Play with Color in Transparent Petals

1 Start EQ5.

2 Choose Create a New Project.

3 Type the name for your new project: C Transparency - Petals.

4 Click OK.

5 Click Worktable — Work on Quilt.

Design the Quilt

Layout

6 Click Quilt — New Quilt — Horizontal.

7 Click the Layout tab along the bottom of the screen.

8 Under Number of blocks, click the arrows to read 1 Horizontal and 1 Vertical.

9 Under Size of blocks, drag the sliders to read 12.00 Width and 12.00 Height.

10 Under Sashing, drag both the sliders to read 0.00 to eliminate the sashing.

Borders

11 Click the Borders tab along the bottom of the screen.

12 Click the Add button twice to make a total of 3 borders.

13 Be sure there is a check next to All under Adjust Size. (Clicking will turn this check on and off.)

14 Click on the inner border and drag one of the sliders to 0.25.

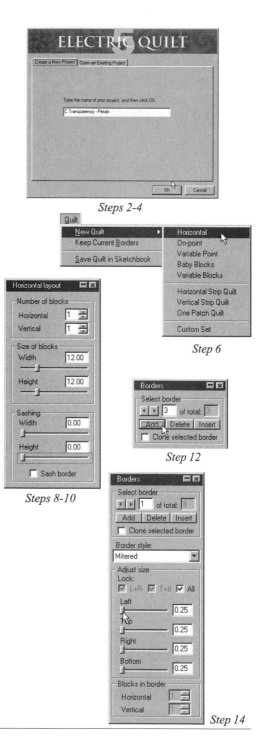

Steps 2-4

Step 6

Steps 8-10

Step 12

Step 14

8

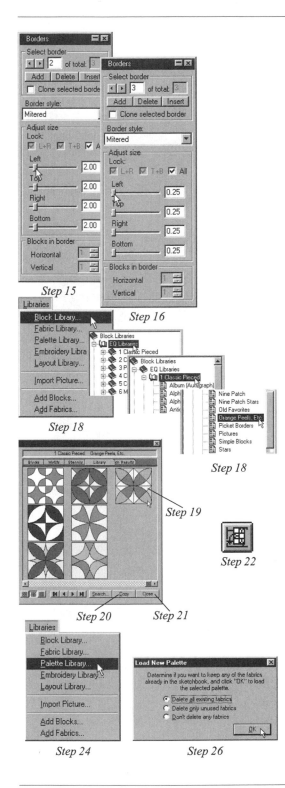

Step 15

Step 16

Step 18

Step 18

Step 19

Step 20 *Step 21*

Step 22

Step 24 *Step 26*

15 Click on the middle border and drag one of the sliders to 2.00.

16 Click on the outer border and drag one of the sliders to 0.25.

17 Click the Layer 1 tab.

Block

18 Click Libraries — Block Library — EQ Libraries — 1 Classic Pieced — Orange Peels. The blocks in this book will appear.

19 Find and click on Spring Beauty. (It is the last block in the Orange Peels category.)

20 Click Copy. You'll notice that the block temporarily disappears, indicating you've copied it into your Sketchbook.

21 Click Close.

22 Click the Set tool, then the Blocks tab.

23 Click the Spring Beauty block to select it, then click in the center of your quilt to set the block.

Collect the Fabrics for the Quilt

24 Click Libraries — Palette Library — EQ5 Palettes tab.

25 Click on the Nursery palette and click Load.

26 Choose "Delete all existing fabrics," and click OK.

8

27 Click Libraries — Palette Library — My Palettes tab.

28 Click on your Pure Colors and Values palette, and click the Load button.

29 Choose "Don't delete any fabrics," and click OK.

30 Click the Spraycan tool (not the EQ4 Spraycan tool).

Color the Quilts

Notice that the quilt has four elements: a center diamond, four flower petals, background, and border. Notice that the four petals overlap the center diamond. You will create transparency where the pieces overlap.

• Use prints only. Tie-dye and washed or marbled prints work beautifully to enhance the illusion.

• Study the quilt as you click each print into place. If the illusion doesn't work, click in a different print. You will see immediately when the illusion is successful.

Quilt 1 - Using Value to Create Transparency

We will work in three values of **red-violet**. Remember: the illusion works best when the colors are of the same saturation (pure colors only or tones only).

31 Make the center diamond a **light value of red-violet**.

32 Make the outer halves of each petal a **dark value of red-violet**.

33 On the inner halves, where the petal overlaps the diamond, insert a **middle value of red-violet**.

34 Make the background **any light color** you like.

35 Use CTRL + click to color the borders with prints you used in the center.

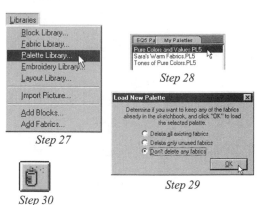

Step 27

Step 28

Step 29

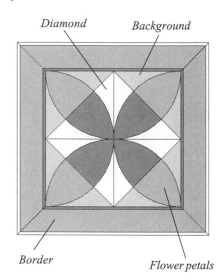

Step 30

Diamond   Background

Border   Flower petals

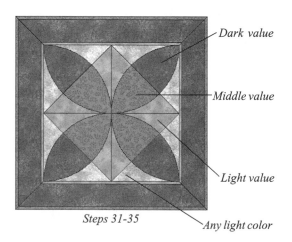

Steps 31-35

Dark value

Middle value

Light value

Any light color

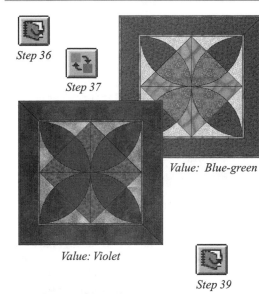

Step 36

Step 37

Value: Blue-green

Value: Violet

Step 39

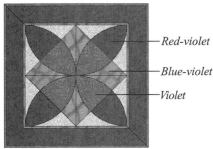

────Red-violet

────Blue-violet

────Violet

Step 40 Analogous: Red-violet

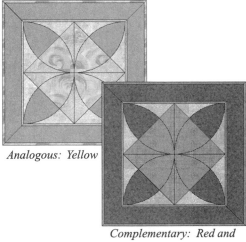

Analogous: Yellow

Complementary: Red and green

36 Save this quilt in the Sketchbook.

More Quilts Using Value
37 Click the Swap tool (not the EQ4 Swap tool).

38 Make two or more quilts using three values of other colors. Don't forget to try one quilt in a value scale of toned fabrics.

39 Save each quilt in the Sketchbook.

Use Harmony and Contrast
40 Make two quilts using analogous colors. Edit your first red-violet quilt to the worktable. To do this, view the Sketchbook, find the quilt and click Edit. Keep the **red-violet** on the outer petals but change to **blue-violet** in the center diamond and **violet** in the inner halves of the petals.

41 Try a second quilt using three other analogous colors.

42 Make one quilt in **red** and **green**, two complements, using a **dark red** in the petals to create the illusion of transparency.

Study your Color Schemes
• Click the View Sketchbook button, then the Quilts tab. Use the arrows to flip through the quilts from first to last.

• At a glance, you can see whether a design is successful and looks transparent. If the illusion does or doesn't work well, try to figure out why.

Remember
• Transparency is one of the few concepts which relies on a formula to achieve the effect.

• It is worth the effort to experiment with transparency because it adds incredible vitality to a quilt.

8

Creating Distance in a Landscape

Color Theory

The colors we use when creating the illusion of distance come from what we see in real life. Foreground colors are strong and vivid. Colors in the distance are vague, muted, and indistinct.

If you want to suggest distance or space, choose muted tones for the distant areas. Since cool colors recede, use them to suggest distance, too. We see an area as if it is far away when it is dull, pale, and blue (even if it is simply a part of an abstract design). Blues suggest sky, and sky is traditionally in the background.

For the foreground, choose strong colors (pure and dark) that attract the eye of the viewer.

Let's Create the Illusion of Distance

1   Start EQ5.

2   Choose Create a New Project.

3   Type the name for your new project: C Distance - Landscape.

4   Click OK.

5   Click Worktable — Work on Quilt.

Design the Quilt

Layout

6   Click Quilt — New Quilt — Horizontal Strip Quilt.

7   Click the Layout tab along the bottom of the screen.

8   Click the Delete button until you have only one strip.

9   Under Strip style, click the dropdown arrow and change it to Pieced Blocks.

10 Under Size of strip, drag the sliders to read 3.00 Width and 72.00 Length.

11 Under Number of blocks, click the arrow to make the blocks along length read 24.

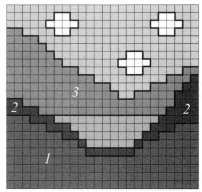

The Blue Ridge Mountains are so named because of the play of misty blues, purples, and greens fading into the distance over multiple mountaintops.

ELECTRIC QUILT

Create a New Project | Open an Existing Project |

Type the name of your project, and then click OK.

C Distance - Landscape

OK   Cancel

Steps 2-4

Quilt

New Quilt ▶   Horizontal
Keep Current Borders   On-point
                         Variable Point
Save Quilt in Sketchbook   Baby Blocks
                         Variable Blocks
Step 6
                         Horizontal Strip Quilt
                         Vertical Strip Quilt
                         One Pa
Custom

Horizontal strip quilt

Select strip
◄ ► 5 of total: 5
Add   Delete   Insert

Step 8

Strip style:
Pieced Blocks ▼

Size of strip
Width
3.00   *Step 10*
Length
72.00

Number of blocks
Along length: 24   *Step 11*
Across width: 1

8

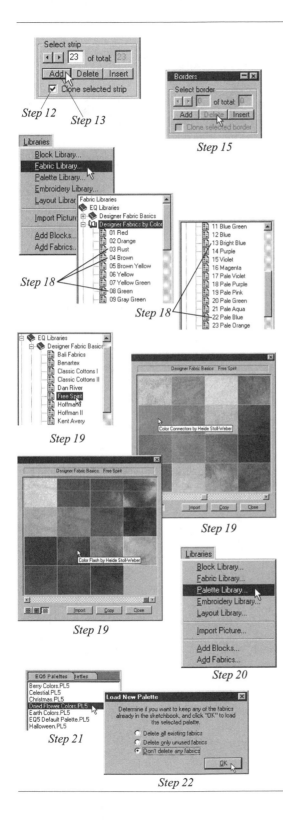

Step 12 *Step 13*

Step 15

Step 18

Step 18

Step 19

Step 19

Step 19

Step 20

Step 21

Step 22

12 Put a check next to Clone selected strip. (Clicking will turn this check on and off.)

13 Click the Add button until you have 23 strips. If you accidentally make 24, click the Delete button once so you have 23 again.

Borders

14 Click the Borders tab.

15 Click the Delete button to eliminate all borders.

16 Click the Layer 1 tab.

Collect Fabrics for the Quilt

We will create a watercolor landscape with prints. The quilt will look best if the prints are tone-on-tone, plain, washed, or if they have small-scale patterns. Be sure to copy these types of fabrics and not busy or large-scaled prints in the next steps.

17 Click Libraries — Fabric Library — EQ Libraries — Designer Fabrics by Color.

18 Copy four fabrics fitting the following descriptions from each of these categories:

03 Rust (very dark rust to brown)
04 Brown (medium to dark brown)
08 Green (vivid, grassy greens)
13 Bright Blue (sky or water-like blues)
22 Pale Blue (pale, cloud-like blues)

19 Scroll up to the top of the Fabric Library list and go to Designer Fabrics Basics — Free Spirit. Hold your cursor over a fabric to see the name. Scroll to the end of this category and copy all the prints (a total of 34) from the Color Connectors and Color Flash lines.

20 Click Libraries — Palette Library — EQ5 Palettes.

21 Click the Dried Flower Colors palette and click Load.

22 Choose "Don't delete any fabrics," and click OK.

8

23 Click Libraries — Palette Library — EQ5 Palettes.

24 Click the Natural Neutrals palette and click Load.

25 Choose "Don't delete any fabrics," and click OK.

26 Click the Swap tool. Click the Prints tab in the palette.

27 Hold your cursor over the edge or corner of the fabrics palette so it turns into an arrow. Then drag the edge or corner out to enlarge the palette to fill the space next to the quilt.

Color the Quilt

You are going to turn the squares into a landscape. Follow the general pattern, but don't worry about how many squares equal a section unless it is mentioned. The picture will not look pictorial until well into the process, so just play and don't worry. It is always changeable. This involves a lot of clicking one square at a time, but since the layout is flexible, you will get more relaxed and free as you work.

To color the Landscape, we will label the bottom row as Row 1 and count upwards.

28 Click on a **pale blue sky** fabric and click to fill the entire quilt.

29 Click the Paintbrush tool.

30 Click on a **dark green** fabric. Hold down your keyboard CTRL key and click in the bottom five rows, Rows 1-5.

31 Click on a **bright, water-like blue**. It will be the lake in the valley. CTRL + click to fill Rows 6-9.

32 Click a **light beige**. CTRL + click in Rows 10 and 11. Warning: This is the last time you should let your finger near the CTRL key.

33 Click the Save in Sketchbook button.

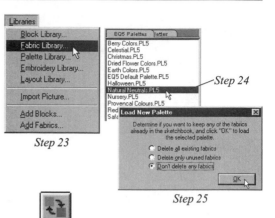

Step 23

Step 24

Step 25

Step 26

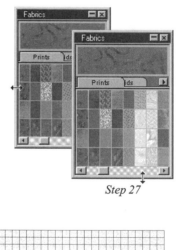

Step 27

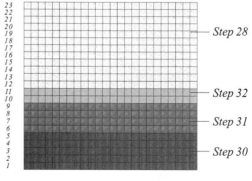

Row

Step 28

Step 32

Step 31

Step 30

Step 33

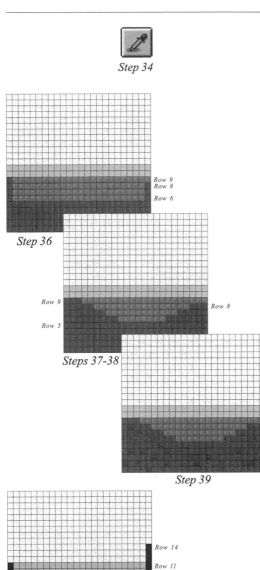

Step 34

Step 36

Row 9
Row 8
Row 6

Row 9
Row 5
Row 8

Steps 37-38

Step 39

Row 14
Row 11
Row 9

Step 41

Row 14
Row 11
Row 5

Step 42

Color Section 1

34 Now to add some interest. Click the Eyedropper tool.

35 Click on the **dark green** fabric in your quilt. The Eyedropper will pick up the green and switch you over to the Paintbrush tool so you can color again.

36 Starting in Row 6 in the outer column on each side, put the dark green 4 squares upward on the left and 3 on the right. (Do not use the CTRL key.)

37 Make a sloping diagonal line from these outer squares down to Row 5 by filling them with the dark green. (Use the pictures as a guide, but do not follow them exactly.)

38 Fill in all the space between Row 5 and the horizon you drew.

39 Choose **at least five other pure and dark greens** (avoid tones) and replace some of the first dark green at random, always maintaining an upward curve from the center to the outer edges. Cluster some fabrics in a few squares in irregular shapes. This will provide variety for the green foreground.

40 Click the Save in Sketchbook button.

Color Section 2 or Rocks in the Foreground

41 Click on a **dark brown** in the palette. Put the dark brown into 2 squares upward from the dark green in the outer left column and into 6 squares upward from the dark green in the outer-right column.

42 Make diagonal lines from these outer squares down to Row 5 by filling them with the **dark brown**. You will cover only the beige and blues, but leave the six center squares in Row 6 blue.

8

43 Fill in all the space between Row 5 and the horizon you drew with the **dark brown**.

44 Choose **several dark browns** and **rusts**, and replace some of the brown squares at random to add variety to the landscape. As you add fabrics, always maintain an upward curve from the center to the outer edges by placing them in diagonal rows. Cluster some fabrics in a few squares in irregular shapes.

45 Fill the squares in Row 5 that are directly under the lake (blue squares) in browns and rusts.

46 Your foreground is now in place. It contains strong, rich dark and pure colors and comes forward visually as things nearby do in reality.

47 Click the Save in Sketchbook button.

Color Section 3 or Background Mountains

48 Click the Eyedropper tool and click on the **light beige** in your quilt. The Eyedropper will pick up the light beige and switch you over to the Paintbrush tool so you can color again.

49 In the outer column on each side, put the light beige up 9 more squares on the left from the dark brown and 1 more on the right from the dark brown. (Do not use the CTRL key.)

50 Make diagonal lines from the outer squares down to the top of the lake (Row 10).

51 Fill in all of the space between your beige diagonal lines and the beige horizon. Color over sky blue, not the brown mountains.

52 Click the Save in Sketchbook button.

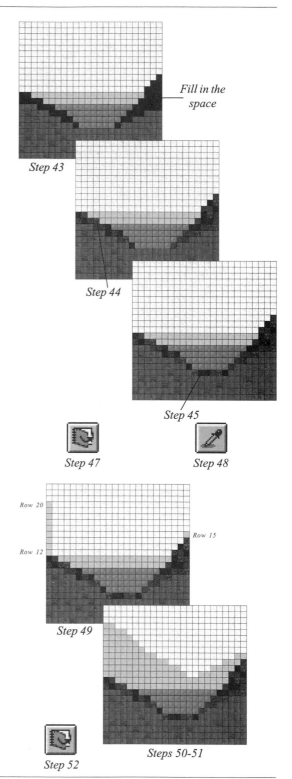

Fill in the space

Step 43

Step 44

Step 45

Step 47   *Step 48*

Row 20

Row 15

Row 12

Step 49

Steps 50-51

Step 52

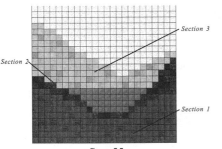

Step 55

Step 56

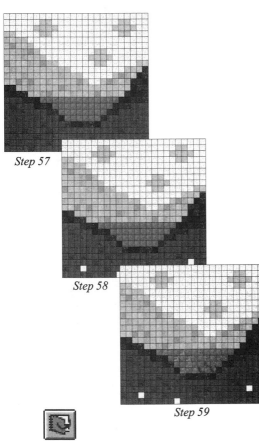

Step 57

Step 58

Step 59

Step 60

53 Click the Eyedropper tool and click on the **blue** of the sky in your quilt. The Eyedropper will pick up the sky-blue and switch you to the Paintbrush tool.

54 Make the center of the beige mountains less of a straight line. Adjust the curve of the beige mountains so that it is only two to three squares high in the center above the lake.

55 Section 3 is also mountainous ground, grass and rocks, but it is in the distance. Therefore, you need to choose **very pale, grayed tones of greens, browns, and rusts**. Also add other cool, dull tones such as **lavenders**. Fill the squares, always maintaining the curve, which dips toward the center from the two sides.

56 Click the Save in Sketchbook button.

Color the Extras

57 Add clouds if you want. They would be white against the blue, but not a pure solid white. Choose a delicate **light blue** print and see how it looks. If you make clouds, make at least 3, two close together on the right and one alone on the left. This will balance the picture.

58 Add flowers to the grassy foreground. Choose a few **rich, pure, warm colors** and scatter them square by square around the green grass. They should remain sparks or accents, so don't add too many.

59 Add waves to the lake if you want. Use a blue very similar to the one already used.

60 Click the Save in Sketchbook button.

8

Add Borders

Coloring the many squares of your landscape quilt was difficult because of their tiny size. Designing with borders before coloring would have made the task even more difficult. But the quilt would look lovely with borders.

61 Click the Borders tab along the bottom of your screen.

62 Click the Add button twice so you have a total of 2 borders.

63 Be sure there is a check next to All under Adjust size. (Clicking will turn this check on and off.)

64 Click the inner border. Drag one of the sliders to 7.00.

65 Click the outer border. Drag one of the sliders to 1.50.

66 Click the Layer 1 tab.

67 Try different colors in the borders and see how they affect the quilt. Save them all in the Sketchbook.

68 Try two shades of a **mellow gold** to imitate a real picture frame.

69 Try two shades of **green**.

70 Try any other colors you want.

71 Save them all in the Sketchbook.

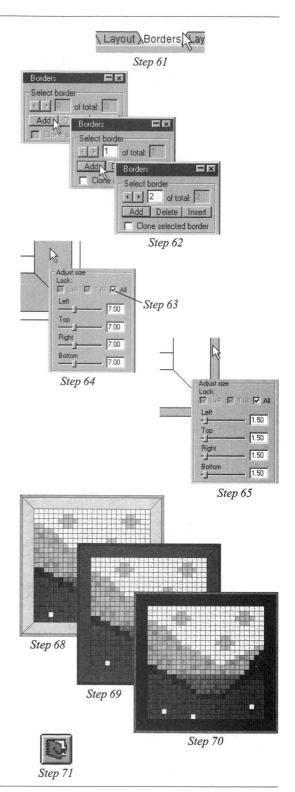

Step 61

Step 62

Step 63

Step 64

Step 65

Step 68

Step 69

Step 70

Step 71

View Sketchbook

Study Your Quilts

Study Your Quilts to See What Colors Dominate and How Background Affects Colors

*   Click the View Sketchbook button and then the Quilts tab.

*   Use the arrows to flip through the saved quilts in order from first to last. This shows the progression as you built up from rows of base colors, adding shape and contrast of color, value and print.

*   Notice how adding a border finishes and acts as a picture frame around the many-pieced quilt.

Remember

*   Things in the distance are cool, dull and pale while things in the foreground are strong in color.

*   Whether they are abstract or realistic, you can use this information to create the illusion of depth in a quilt.

8

Luminosity Creates Shimmer and Glow

Color Theory

Some quilts, as some paintings, seem luminous; in other words they glow. The effect of luminosity is an illusion, and to achieve the illusion, you play with contrast using these color concepts you already know:

- **Value**: Light against dark

- **Intensity**: Pure against toned

- **Temperature**: Warm against cool

- **Proportion**: Little accents against lots of background

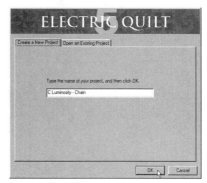

Let's Play with Luminosity

1 Start EQ5.

2 Choose Create a New Project.

3 Type the name for your new project: C Luminosity - Chain.

4 Click OK.

5 Click Worktable — Work on Quilt.

Design the Quilt

Layout

6 Click Quilt — New Quilt — Horizontal.

7 Click the Layout tab along the bottom of the screen.

8 Under Number of blocks, click the arrows to read 5 Horizontal and 5 Vertical.

9 Under Size of blocks, drag the sliders to read 8.00 Width and 8.00 Height.

10 Under Sashing, drag both sliders to read 0.00 to eliminate the sashing.

Steps 2-4

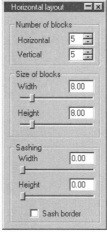

Steps 8-10

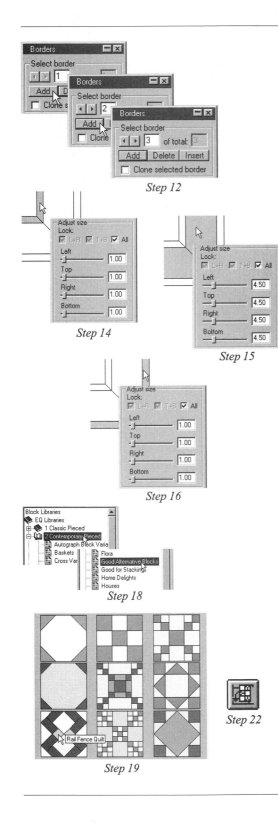

Step 12

Step 14

Step 15

Step 16

Step 18

Step 19

Step 22

Borders

11 Click the Borders tab along the bottom of the screen.

12 Click Add twice to make a total of three borders.

13 Be sure there is a check next to All under Adjust Size. (Clicking will turn this check on and off.)

14 Click on the inner border. Make sure all sides are 1.00.

15 Click on the middle border. Drag one of the sliders to 4.50. All sides will adjust automatically.

16 Click on the outer border. Make sure all sides are 1.00.

17 Click the Layer 1 tab along the bottom of the screen.

Block

18 Click Libraries – Block Library – EQ Libraries – 2 Contemporary Pieced – Good Alternative Blocks.

19 Find and click on the Rail Fence Quilt block in the first column.

20 Click Copy. You'll notice that the block temporarily disappears, indicating you've "copied" it into your Sketchbook.

21 Click Close. Now you're back to the quilt worktable and ready to set blocks.

22 Click the Set tool. The Blocks palette will appear showing the Rail Fence Quilt block.

23 Click on the block. Position your mouse cursor over any block on your empty quilt layout, hold down your keyboard CTRL key and click. The Rail Fence Quilt block now fills the quilt.

8

Select Fabrics for the Quilt

24 Click Libraries — Palette Library — EQ5 Palettes.

25 Choose the Celestial palette.

26 Click the Load button.

27 Choose "Delete all existing fabrics," then click OK.

28 Click Libraries — Palette Library — My Palettes.

29 Choose your Pure Colors and Values palette.

30 Click the Load button.

31 Choose "Don't delete any fabrics," then click OK.

32 In addition, you need to select a variety of warm colored fabrics in bright or pure yellows, oranges, and reds.

33 Click Libraries — Fabric Library — EQ Libraries — Designer Fabric Basics.

34 Choose four to six tie-dye-looking fabrics from each of these fabric collections:

- Bali Fabrics
- Classic Cottons I
- Free Spirit
- Hoffman I

To do this, drag the horizontal scrollbar to the right to see all the fabrics in the collection. When you find one you like, click on the fabric swatch to select it and click Copy.

35 Click the Close button when you are finished.

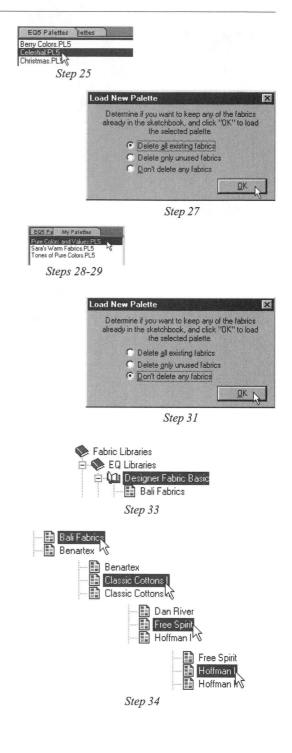

Step 25

Step 27

Steps 28-29

Step 31

Step 33

Step 34

Step 36

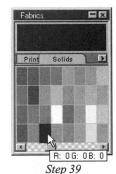

Step 37   *Step 39*

Steps 39-42

Step 44

Step 45

36 Click the Paintbrush tool. The EQ fabric palette will appear.

37 Click on the Prints tab in the palette. Scroll to the right to see the fabrics available. The fabrics you added with appear on the far right.

Color the Quilt

38 Look at the quilt block for color placement. You will see that the design can be colored to look like twisted ribbon. We will color the ribbon first.

39 Put a solid **black** in the spaces shown. To do this, click on the Solids tab at the top of your fabric palette. Scroll to find black and click on it. Hold down the CTRL key on your keyboard and click in the upwards-facing ribbon sections. You will be coloring two parts: the ribbon side and the crossover squares. When you are done, the two pieces will look like one piece.

40 CTRL + click in the inner and outer borders to color them **black**.

41 Click on a **solid dark gray** (the swatch after the black) in the palette.

42 Use CTRL + click to color the downwards-facing ribbon sections (pieces shown in gray), using the same method.

43 Click on the Prints tab in the palette.

44 Click the Swap tool.

45 Consider all of the on-point square patches in the quilt to be background. Consider the corner triangles of each block to be background also, since they form squares when more than one block is placed side by side. Fill these background squares and middle border with a **light, grayed blue**.

8

46 Sit back and look at your blue, gray and black quilt. Dull, isn't it? Let's brighten it up! But first, save it in the Sketchbook.

Step 46   Step 47

47 Click the Paintbrush tool. Now you will replace some of the dull blue squares with **bright, warm yellows, oranges and reds**.

48 Use a variety of fabrics. Begin by placing several of the brightest and strongest in the center of the quilt. Scatter others randomly around the quilt. Move them, repeat them, and scatter them, always working from the center out and filling only 1/3 of the squares with the bright colors. *You are aiming for a black quilt with sparks of random warm color.* Leave the gray-blue in the outer squares and triangles and scattered in between the warm colors.

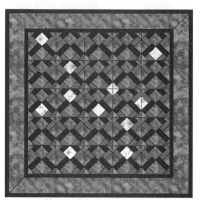

Steps 48-49

As you drop warm colors into the quilt, you will see how it comes to life and how the colors glow behind the ribbon grid. This is how you create the illusion of luminosity: combine a few light or pure, warm colors with a lot of dark, toned, cool colors.

Play with the Borders

49 Leave the inner and outer borders black and change the middle border. Try different warm colors from the center. Notice how the quilt changes as you change the borders.

50 Save the quilts you find interesting in the Sketchbook.

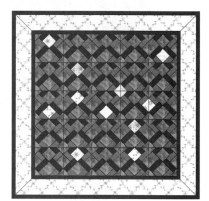

Step 49

Play with the Background

51 Click the Solids tab in the fabric palette. Use CTRL + click to change the gray ribbon sections to a **solid, dull, dark purple**. Keep your eyes on the quilt as you drop in the color and notice how the simple addition of color, even though dark, brightens up the quilt.

52 Save this quilt in the Sketchbook.

Step 52

Step 51

Steps 54-55

Step 56

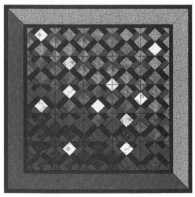

Step 58

Step 59

Step 61

53 Click the Prints tab.

54 Change the background squares on the lower-left of the quilt to a **dark, dull blue**. Use a variety of dark blue prints. Replace, working inward and upward. Warning: You cannot use the CTRL + click method. You need to color square by square or you will lose all of your warm colors. Notice how the dark blue makes the light, bright warm colors glow even more than the original medium blue.

55 Change the middle border to match the **dark blue** background. Notice that this increases the illusion of glow or luminosity.

56 Add some **medium dull blue** fabrics in the center of the quilt and **light dull blue** fabrics in the top-right corner, so the background goes from dark blue at the bottom-left gradually to light blue at the top-right. This will make the quilt richer.

57 Save this quilt in the Sketchbook.

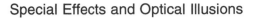

Step 57

8

58 To add more interest, change the top and right side of the middle border to a **light dull blue** you used. Change the bottom and left side of the middle border to a **dark to medium dull blue** you used.

59 Save this quilt in the Sketchbook.

Add More Shining Light

60 Return to any quilt and add more scattered warm colors. To do this, click the View Sketchbook button, then the Quilts tab. Use the arrows to scroll through the quilts. When you find one you wish to add more warm colors to, click the Edit button.

61 Click the Paintbrush tool. Click a **warm color** in the palette and click to add more scattered warm colors in the background squares.

62 Try a **lighter yellow** near the bottom-left of your quilt, and the same yellow near the top-right of your quilt. Notice how if the contrast is low, the colors shimmer; if the contrast is high, the colors glow.

63 Try using warm colors from the center in the inner and outer borders.

64 Save any new quilts in the Sketchbook.

Steps 61-62

Study Your Quilts to See What Colors Glow and How Background Affects Colors

- Click the View Sketchbook button, then the Quilts tab. Use the arrows to flip through the saved quilts in order from first to last.

- This overview of the finished quilts gives you a wealth of identical designs changed only by color displaying how color affects quilt design.

- Notice how the simple gray quilt becomes richer as you first add warm bright colors and then dark, dull, cool colors and change the borders.

Remember What You Practiced

- The effect of luminosity is an illusion, and it is achievable.

- To achieve a luminous effect, you play with contrast of value, intensity, temperature and proportion.

- A luminous, glowing color scheme is created by combining light, bright colors with dull, dark colors.

- The dark, dull colors act as background for the light, bright colors, which then appear to glow.

Step 63

Step 64

Study Your Quilts

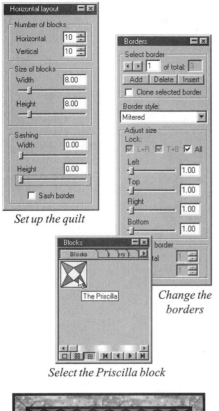

Set up the quilt

Change the borders

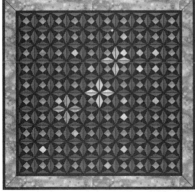

Select the Priscilla block

Use the principles of luminosity to make the center diamonds, or even stars, shimmer on the dull background

- Proportion: Try small areas of bright pure colors surrounded by large areas of dark dull colors.

- If the contrast is low, the colors shimmer; if the contrast is high, the colors glow.

More Practice with Luminosity

- Start a new 10x10 horizontal quilt that has 8.00x8.00 blocks and no sashing.

- Make three mitered borders at 1.00, 5.75, and 1.00 sizes.

- Search for the Priscilla block in the Library and set this in every square.

- CTRL + click to color the inner and outer borders, as well as the four star points in every block a solid black.

- Start with a light blue-gray in all other sections. Then, slowly shade the quilt from dark blue in the bottom-left corner to light blue in the top-right corner.

- Choose your bright, warm yellows, oranges, and reds and set those in your quilt. Try setting light yellows in the dark bottom-left corner of the quilt and watch how they glow. Replace them with medium yellows and watch how they shimmer now that the contrast has changed.

8

Combining Color Effects and the Lines of Design

Color Theory

Traditionally, artists use a particular color for one of three reasons: its visual effect, its emotional effect, or its symbolic effect.

Let's see what this means. Consider red, for example. The artist might use red because it is bright and attracts the eye of the viewer. That is its visual effect. Or, she might use red because it is exciting and stimulating. That is its emotional effect. Then again, she might use it because it symbolizes courage, a message she wants to convey. That is its symbolic effect.

You may be inclined to use a color for one effect more than another. And you probably will use colors for different purposes, at different times, in different quilts. But knowing what the effects of a color are and that these effects are interrelated helps you to convey the mood or message you want in your quilt.

We can use this knowledge of general color effects to make our quilts do what we want them to do. After all, we want our quilts to have meaning when we are finished. We usually have a purpose in mind for each quilt. We want it to lift someone's spirits or be a showstopper, to sooth or intrigue. We must first recognize what effect we are striving to achieve, and then we can decide how to get there from here.

Use Colors for Visual Effects

It's fun to be aware of and use colors for their visual effects.

Use Colors for Emotional Effects

Colors affect mood. There is established scientific evidence to verify how colors affect people. Psychologists have gotten us to brighten our hospitals, schools, children's rooms, and clothing precisely for this reason. To the right are the moods different colors evoke, according to several color experts.

Use Colors for Visual Effects

- The blues and greens are soothing and relaxing, light and airy.

- Yellows convey weightlessness and seem to float.

- Reds and oranges are stimulating and agitating. They attract the eye.

- Pure colors convey a feeling of buoyancy.

- Muted colors convey stability and seriousness.

Use Colors for Emotional Effects

- Blue — placidity, relaxation, passiveness, coldness

- Red — excitement, agitation, animation, passion, gravity

- Green — tranquility, hope, decay, jealousy

- Yellow — buoyancy, thoughtfulness, aggressiveness

- Pure colors — buoyancy

- Pastel colors — gracefulness, light, airiness

Notice from the list on the previous page that the mood a color conveys can vary. For example, yellow may be buoyant or aggressive, and green may be tranquil or jealous. Mood from color is subjective. The mood depends on the viewer's experiences and preferences, as well as the context in which the quilter places the color. Yet, in general, certain moods are evoked by certain colors.

Use Colors to Convey Seasons and Time

Use Colors to Convey Seasons and Time

- Seasons — Spring, Summer, Fall, Winter

- Times of Day — Dawn, Morning, Afternoon, Evening, Night

- Weather — Rain, Fog, Sun, Wind, Heat, Cold

Look at the list to the left and consider which colors are associated with which season, time of day, or type of weather.

Use Colors Symbolically

One of the most fascinating aspects of color is its symbolic meaning. Color has played a part in man's symbolism for thousands of years. We learn the symbolic meanings of colors in our culture as children, and use them unconsciously all of our lives. Some are from nature, some from years of tradition. In different cultures, colors may convey different ideas, but in Western culture, colors have the symbolic meanings listed to the left.

Use Colors Symbolically

- Blue — sky, heaven, water

- Green — water, hope, spring, renewal — or jealousy and fear *(these are poisonous emotions and come from the fact that arsenic manufactured in ancient times was green and used to poison enemies)*

- Red — blood, courage, sacrifice

- Black — death, the underworld, mourning, desolation

- White — purity, chastity — or surrender, cowardice

- Yellow — sun, wealth — or envy, treachery, cowardice

- Purple — royalty, authority

- Gray — rain, fog, depression, dreariness

Colors affect us at their symbolic level because, within our culture, we are all familiar with their connotations. Patriotic quilts in red, white, and blue are examples of the symbolic use of color. Wedding quilts; anniversary quilts; commemorative quilts honoring states or cities, schools or churches; all are examples of places we might use color for symbolic meaning above other considerations.

8

Color and Shape

We can't isolate our use of color from the lines of the design. We have been concentrating on color and how it affects our quilts, but actually color, line, and shape support each other. Quilters rely on shapes all the time; they are our mainstay. Usually, they are our reason for making a quilt. Being aware of the power of shape combined with color will enable you to create dynamic and unified quilts.

Shapes Convey Feelings and Moods

Quilters of today are consciously using the symbolism of shape and color to make beautiful quilts. Although the ideas may be new to you, try applying them to quilts you see in shows and magazines. Study the quilts that have the greatest impact on you and see how the quiltmakers consciously used their knowledge of color and shape to elicit a desired response from their audience.

Combine Color & Shape for Visual Effects

Let's play with some simple quilt designs to see how powerful a color scheme can be.

1   Start EQ5.

2   Choose Create a New Project.

3   Type the name for your new project: C Combining Color and Shape.

4   Click OK.

5   Click Worktable — Work on Quilt.

Design Quilt 1: Horizontal Cool Stripes

Layout

6   Click Quilt — New Quilt — Horizontal.

7   Click the Layout tab along the bottom of the screen.

Shapes Convey Feelings and Moods

• Just as blues are soothing and relaxing colors, so are horizontal lines. Circles and S-shaped curves are graceful and soothing, so are evenly spaced, spread-out designs.

• Red, on the other hand, is an exciting, agitating color. Broken, staccato lines and jagged edges are as well. These shapes affect the viewer's mood.

• Toned-down colors are calming and stable. Vertical lines, perfectly balanced forms, and squares suggest stability and dignity.

• Dome-shaped designs, arches, and pure colors all produce buoyant effects.

• Horizontal lines denote weight and distance while vertical lines soar into lightness and height.

• Diagonal lines, of course, force the eye to travel across the quilt and give it movement.

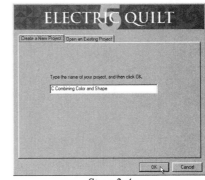

Steps 2-4

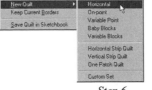

Step 6

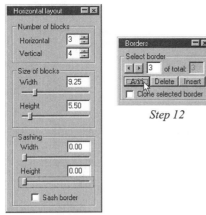

Steps 8-10

Step 12

Step 14

Step 15

Step 16

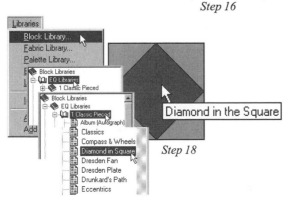

Step 18

8 Under Number of blocks, click the arrows to read 3 Horizontal and 4 Vertical.

9 Under Size of blocks, drag the sliders to read 9.25 Width and 5.50 Height.

10 Under Sashing, drag both the sliders to read 0.00.

Borders

11 Click the Borders tab along the bottom of the screen.

12 Click the Add button twice to make a total of 3 borders.

13 Be sure there is a check next to All under Adjust Size. (Clicking will turn this check on and off.)

14 Click on the inner border. Drag one of the sliders to 0.75. All sides will adjust automatically.

15 Click on the middle border. Drag one of the sliders to read 1.50.

16 Click on the outer border. Drag one of the sliders to read 0.50.

17 Click the Layer 1 tab along the bottom of the screen.

Blocks

18 You will collect four blocks for this lesson. Go to Libraries — Block Library — EQ Libraries — 1 Classic Pieced — Diamond in Square. Click on and copy the first Diamond in the Square block in this category.

8

19 Go to the 2 Contemporary Pieced — Strip Quilts category. Click on and copy the Random Stripes block. (If your view is still set to 9 blocks at a time, it is the middle block in the bottom row.)

20 Go to 3 Paper Piecing — Geometrics. Click on and copy the Rail Fence III block.

21 Go to 4 Classic Appliqué — Folk Art Blocks. Click on and copy the Wreath Stencil block.

22 Click Close.

23 Click the Set tool. The four blocks will appear.

24 Click on the Random Stripes block in the palette and CTRL + click in one square on your quilt. All squares will fill with fully colored Random Stripes.

25 Click the Rotate tool.

26 CTRL + click once on any block. All blocks will rotate. You now have a quilt of random width horizontal stripes.

Collect the Fabrics

27 Click Libraries — Palette Library — My Palettes tab.

28 Click on and load the Tones of Pure Colors palette.

29 Choose "Delete all existing fabrics," and click OK.

30 Click Libraries — Palette Library — My Palettes tab.

31 Click on and load the Pure Colors and Values palette.

32 Choose "Don't delete any fabrics," and click OK.

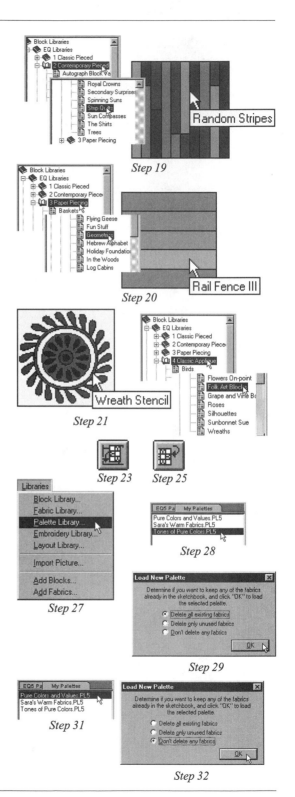

Step 19

Step 20

Step 21

Step 23   *Step 25*

Step 27

Step 28

Step 29

Step 31

Step 32

Step 33

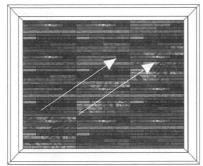

Step 35 — Color randomly on the diagonals from bottom-left to top-right

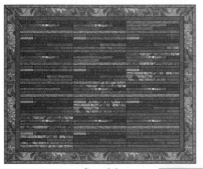

Step 36

Step 37

33 Click the Paintbrush tool, then the Prints tab in the palette.

Color the Quilt

34 Color the Random Stripes blocks in many values of blue. Start by CTRL + clicking to recolor each block the same way.

35 Choose a different **blue** fabric. Color randomly up a diagonal line across your quilt without using the CTRL key. Just scatter the fabric quickly from the bottom-left to upper-right of the quilt. Don't worry about where you're clicking, and just do one pass across your quilt. Choose another fabric. Color in one pass across your quilt along a higher or lower diagonal. Repeat, using each new fabric in multiple and varied positions. Use a small amount of blue-violets and violets as accents.

36 Color the borders to emphasize the colors in the center.

37 Save this quilt in the Sketchbook.

Look at your quilt. You have combined cool colors with horizontal stripes to create a soothing, relaxing design.

Design Quilt 2: Vertical Hot Stripes
Layout

38 Click the Layout tab along the bottom of your screen.

39 Under Number of blocks, click the arrows to read 4 Horizontal and 4 Vertical.

40 Under Size of blocks, drag the sliders to read 7.75 Width and 11.50 Height.

41 Under Sashing, leave the sliders at 0.00.

Borders

42 Click the Borders tab along the bottom of the screen.

43 Leave the number of borders at 3.

Steps 39-41

8

44 Be sure there is a check next to All under Adjust Size. (Clicking will turn this check on and off.)

45 Leave the inner border at 0.75.

46 Click on the middle border. Drag one of the sliders to read 3.75.

47 Click on the outer border. Drag one of the sliders to read 0.75.

48 Click the Layer 1 tab along the bottom of the screen. If you are missing blocks in the fourth column, we will fix that in Steps 51 and 52.

49 Click the Rotate tool.

50 CTRL + click on any block to rotate the stripes so they are vertical.

Skip Steps 51 and 52 if you already have blocks in the fourth column.

51 Click the Set tool.

52 Click on the Random Stripes block in the palette and CTRL + click to fill the remaining squares with blocks. You now have a simple design of vertical stripes.

Color the Quilt

53 Click the Swap tool.

54 Replace the blues in the Random Stripes blocks and borders with many values of strong, **bright red**, **orange** and **yellow**. Use only a small amount of the yellow as accents.

55 Click the Paintbrush tool. Click without the CTRL key using different fabrics in multiple and varied positions on a diagonal from the bottom-left to upper-right.

56 Recolor the borders to emphasize the colors in the center if needed.

57 Save the quilt in the Sketchbook.

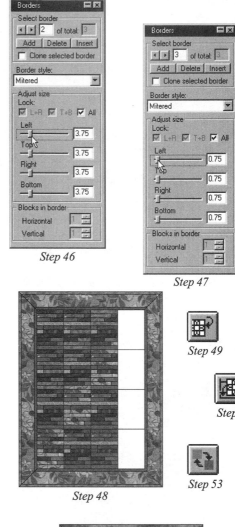

Step 46

Step 47

Step 49

Step 51

Step 53

Step 48

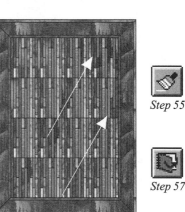

Step 55

Step 57

Steps 54-56

Step 58

Steps 60-62

Step 64

Steps 67-68

Step 66

Step 69

Step 71

Look at your quilt. You have combined warm colors with vertical stripes to create a vibrant, stimulating design.

Quilt 3: Make a New Quilt with Circles and Stripes

Layout

58 Click Quilt — New Quilt — Horizontal.

59 Click the Layout tab along the bottom of the screen.

60 Under Number of blocks, click the arrows to read 5 Horizontal and 5 Vertical.

61 Under Size of blocks, drag the sliders to read 12.00 Width and 12.00 Height.

62 Under Sashing, drag both the sliders to read 0.00.

Borders

63 Click the Borders tab along the bottom of the screen.

64 Click the Add button twice so you have a total of 3 borders.

65 Be sure there is a check next to All under Adjust Size. (Clicking will turn this check on and off.)

66 Click on the inner border. Drag one of the sliders to read 0.75.

67 Click on the middle border. Under Border style, change it to Corner Blocks.

68 Drag one of the sliders to read 12.00.

69 Click on the outer border and drag one of the sliders to read 0.75.

70 Click the Layer 1 tab along the bottom of the screen.

8

Blocks

71 Click the Set tool. The four blocks will appear.

72 Click on the Rail Fence III block in the palette and CTRL + click in one square in the quilt. All squares will fill with the Rail Fence III block, forming horizontal stripes across the quilt.

73 Still with the Set tool, find the Wreath Stencil block in the palette and click on it.

74 You are going to replace five Rail Fence III blocks with the Wreath Stencil block. Columns are numbered from left to right and rows from top to bottom. Click block by block to place it in:

Column 1 row 4
Column 2 row 2
Column 3 row 1
Column 4 row 3
Column 5 row 5
Bottom-right corner of the middle border

Color the Quilt

75 Click the Paintbrush tool.

76 Start with the Rail Fence III blocks. Color the quilt in **strong, pure, and bright blues, blue-violets, and violets**. The Watercolor fabrics will work well here. Begin by CTRL + clicking to color all the blocks the same way. Then click without the CTRL key to vary the values and the positions of colors along the diagonal to create movement across the quilt.

77 Color the borders, including the corner blocks, so they enhance the colors in the center stripes.

78 CTRL + click to color all wreaths in the same cool colors. You may also use black for part of the wreath.

79 Vary the backgrounds of the wreath blocks.

80 Save the quilt in the Sketchbook.

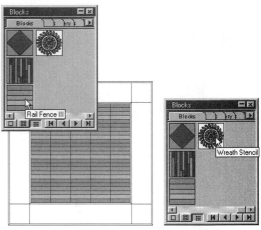

Step 72   *Step 73*

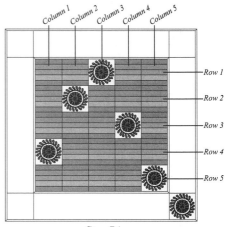

Step 74

Step 75

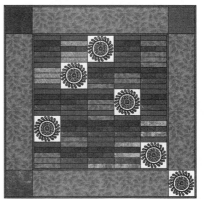

Step 80

Steps 76-79

8

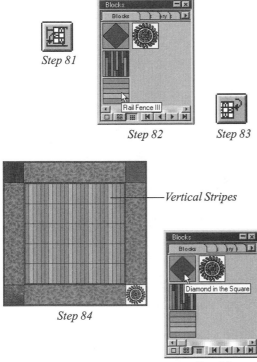

Step 81

Step 82   *Step 83*

Vertical Stripes

Step 84

Step 85

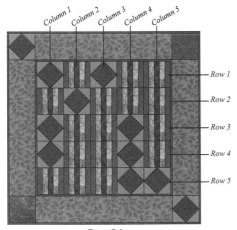

Step 86

Step 87

Look at the cool quilt. You have combined color, horizontal stripes and circles to create a restful and graceful quilt.

Quilt 4: Hot Stripes & Squares

81 Click the Set tool.

82 Click on the Rail Fence III block in the palette. CTRL + click to fill all blocks in the current quilt with stripes.

83 Click the Rotate tool.

84 CTRL + click on one block to rotate all blocks, so the stripes are vertical.

85 Still using the Set tool, click on the Diamond in the Square block in the palette.

86 You are going to replace some Rail Fence III blocks with the Diamond in the Square block. Columns are numbered from left to right and rows from top to bottom. Click block by block to place it in:

Column 1 rows 1, 3, and 4
Column 2 row 2
Column 3 row 1
Column 4 row 3, 4, 5
Column 5 row 5
Top-left and bottom-right corners of the middle border

Color the Quilt

87 Click the Paintbrush tool.

88 Color the quilt in **strong, pure and bright reds**, **oranges and yellows**. Prints with very little pattern to no pattern at all look the best, so copy more fabrics from the Fabric Library of you think the current fabrics are too textured. CTRL + click to color all the Rail Fence III blocks the same way. CTRL + click to color all the Diamond in the Square blocks the same way.

8

89 Color the borders to enhance the colors in the center stripes.

90 Click without holding down the CTRL key to vary the values and the positions of colors in the Rail Fence III block. Color along the diagonal in various warm values to create movement across the quilt.

91 Vary the centers of the Diamond in the Square blocks while keeping their outer corners the same.

92 Save this quilt in the Sketchbook.

Look at the hot quilt. You have combined warm colors, vertical stripes and squares to create an exciting and vibrant quilt.

Quilt 5: Peaceful Stripes & Squares in Quiet Colors

93 Click the Swap tool.

94 Replace the warm colors with **grayed tones of cool and warm colors**. The Watercolor fabrics will work best here.

95 Now to add some detail! Click the Paintbrush tool. Vary the values and the positions of colors to create movement across the quilt.

96 Color the borders to enhance the colors in the center stripes.

97 Vary the centers of the Diamond in the Square blocks but keep the outer corners the same.

98 Save the quilt in the Sketchbook.

Look at the quilt. Notice how the muted colors soften the design and give it a stable, calm feeling.

8

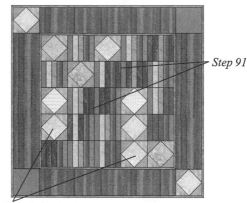

Step 91

Step 90

Step 92   Step 93

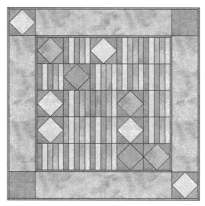

Step 97

Step 98

View Sketchbook

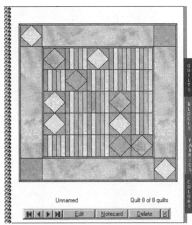

Unnamed   Quilt 8 of 8 quilts

View your quilts in the Sketchbook

Log Cabin - Rotary Ribbon

Lightening Strips

Mexican Blanket

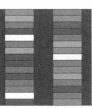

Roman Stripe

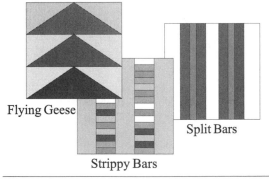

Flying Geese

Split Bars

Strippy Bars

Study Your Quilts

- Click the View Sketchbook button, then the Quilts tab. Use the arrows to flip through a slide show of all the quilts.

- Notice how different the cool and warm quilts look.

- Notice how adding a block in the border pulls the eye outward to include the border, and also adds a touch of surprise, bringing out the center design.

Remember

- As you plan your next quilt, remember to consciously consider how color and shape can combine to enhance any effect you want to achieve.

- You have made only five quilts and played just a little with the ideas of combining color and shape for special effects. Quilts, with their myriad of design possibilities, are perfect places to experiment with this color concept.

Suggestions For Further Practice

- Set up your own quilt layout and use the ideas presented in the lesson introduction under "Shapes Convey Feelings and Moods" to help you choose your blocks. For example, use blues and S-shaped curves together, or arches and the pure colors. If you need more blocks with stripes, use the Block Library's Search tool to find them. Here are just a few striped blocks in the EQ Libraries to consider:

  Log Cabins (any)

  Flying Geese (any)

  Mexican Blanket

  Lightening Strips

  Split Bars

  Strippy Bars

  Roman Stripe

8

CHAPTER 7

Perspective and Dimension Through Light and Shadow

Value adds depth to a Thousand Pyramids

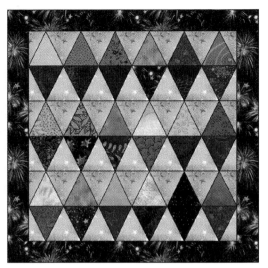

Pure and bright colors advance on a pale background, creating a floating effect

Value enhances the illusion of perspective in an Attic Window

Attic Windows are the perfect opportunity for scrap quilts

PAGES 176 & 180

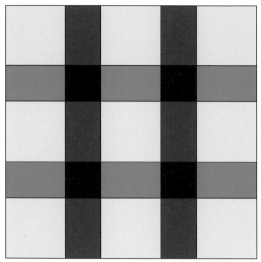

Two complements appear darker where they overlap

Transparency Formula 1: Three values of one color

Transparency Formula 2: Three analogous colors

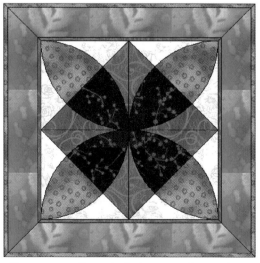

Transparency Formula 3: Any two colors and one value

PAGES 186 & 196

CHAPTER 8
Optical Illusions

Strong colors in the foreground and pale tones in the background create the illusion of distance

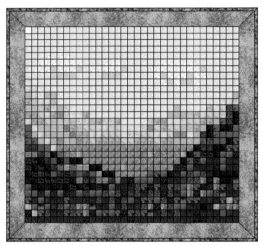

Use borders to frame your quilt as you would a piece of artwork

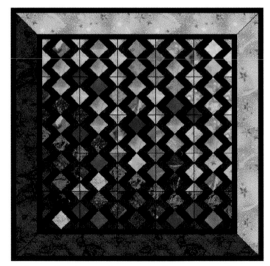

Create luminosity by surrounding scattered pure, warm colors with dark, cool colors

Echo the warm colors in the narrow borders to enhance the quilt

PAGES 200 & 208

CHAPTER 8
Color Effects and the Lines of Design

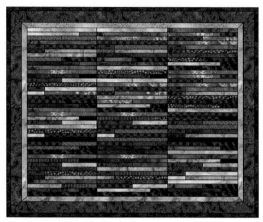

Combine cool blues and horizontal lines to create a restful quilt design

Horizontal lines and soothing circles (scattered for movement) create a peaceful design

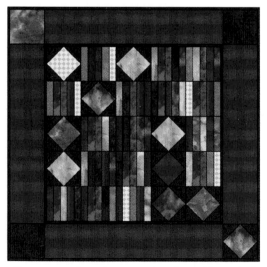

Use warm reds and oranges together with vertical lines to create a vibrant, stimulating design

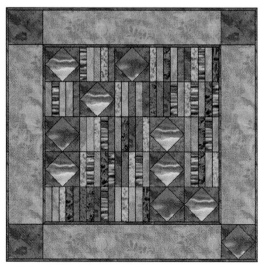

Calm down the same design using tones of warm and cool colors

PAGE 216

Appendix

EQ Blocks to Use for Different Effects

After you do the lessons in this book, you may want to try more difficult and original designs. Below are listed just some of the blocks that lend themselves to different color concepts. Blocks which contain overlapping designs are perfect for transparency. Blocks which contain two-sided designs are perfect for light and shadow. Some blocks contain strips or rings that are great for gradations.

Use them or search the library for other choices. You will learn a great deal from simply scrolling through the library and analyzing the blocks. The amazing array of blocks already provided can keep you busy with color effects for quite a long time. I hope!

EQ Libraries	1	Classic Pieced
	2	Contemporary Pieced
	3	Paper Pieced
	4	Classic Applique

Transparency

Block Name	EQ Library	Book
Mosaic, No. 2	1	Antique Mosaics
Mosaic, No. 4	1	Antique Mosaics
Mosaic, No. 5	1	Antique Mosaics
Ohio Star	1	Classics
Transparent Circle	1	Compass & Wheels
Chariot Wheel	1	Compass & Wheels
King's Crown	1	Diamond in Square
Contrary Wife	1	Diamond in Square
Odds and Ends	1	Eccentrics
Four X Star	1	Five Patch
Album Quilt	1	Five Patch
Girl's Favorite	1	Four Patch
Arbor Window	1	Nine Patch
Summer Winds	1	Nine Patch
Spring Beauty	1	Orange Peels, Etc.
Boise	1	Traditional 4X
Cross 4	2	Cross Variations
Diamond Diane's Fan	2	Fans
Leaf Fan	2	Fans
Rose Window	2	Kaleidoscopes
Dunce Caps	2	Kaleidoscopes
Windmill	2	Secondary Surprises

Color Wheels

Block Name	EQ Library	Book
Any Compass	1	Compasses & Wheels
Any 3 Petal Dresden Fan	1	Dresden Fan
12 Point Star	1	Stars
Rainbow Fan	2	Fans
One Wheel with 12 Spokes	2	Pinwheels & Potpourri
Three Wheels with 12 Spokes	2	Pinwheels & Potpourri
Five Wheel with 12 Spokes	2	Pinwheels & Potpourri

Depth, Light and Shadow

Birds in Air	1	Classics
Attic Window	1	Classics
Ribbons	1	Eccentrics
Slashed Album	1	Eccentrics
Workbox	1	Eccentrics
Jewel	1	Eccentrics
Star of the East	1	Eight-Point Stars
St. Louis Star	1	Five Patch
Four Patch	1	Four Patch
Lattice Square	1	Four Patch
Blue Boutonnieres	1	Four Patch
Baton Rouge	1	Ladies Art Company
Chinese Lantern	1	Old Favorites
Jewel Star	1	Old Favorites
The Spool	1	Simple Blocks
The Diversion Quilt	1	Simple Blocks
Attic Window	1	Simple Blocks
Split 12 Point Star	1	Stars
Purple Coneflower	1	Stars
Costume Jewelry	2	Pinwheels & Potpourri
Perspective Grid 2	2	Pinwheels & Potpourri

Gradation of Any Kind

Block Name	EQ Library	Book
Mosaic No. 17	1	Antique Mosaics
Log Cabin	1	Classics
Log Cabin (2)	1	Classics
Wild Goose Chase	1	Classics
Pineapple	1	Old favorites
Wild Goose Chase *(Several)*	1	Simple Blocks
Four X Variation	1	Simple Blocks
Any Strip Quilt	2	Strip Quilts
Any Pineapples	3	Pineapples
Interlocking Squares	5	Tile & Celtic Designs
Interlocking Rings	5	Tile & Celtic Designs

How Colors Behave/Color Strength

Square in a Square	1	Diamond in Square
Bird's Nest	1	Five Patch
Carrie Nation Quilt	1	Four Patch
Schoolgirl's Puzzle	1	Four Patch
DoubleX, No. 4	1	Ladies Art Company
Wyoming Valley	1	Nine Patch

Effects Colors Have on Each Other

Action	Effect
Use an achromatic color scheme	easy, safe, can be dull
Use a monochromatic color scheme	easy, safe, soothing
Use an analogous color scheme	easy, safe, soothing
Use a polychromatic color scheme	exciting, active
Use cool colors	calm, soothing
Use warm colors	stimulating, exciting
Use warm and cool colors together	strong, exciting
Use warm colors in the background	it becomes foreground
Use cool colors in the foreground	it becomes background
Use complements together	stimulating, strong
Use complements equally	vibrating, hard to look at
Use complements unequally	strong but harmonious
Use pure colors	strong, exciting
Use toned colors	soft, soothing
Use light and dark values right next to each other	strong, vibrant
Go gradually from light to dark values	softens contrast
Use several kinds of contrast together	strong, vibrant
Use gray with a color	it takes on the cast of the complement
Combine color and shape	emphasizes effect of both
Echo a color in the background	balances
Add gray or separate colors with gray	neutralizes, softens
Add neutrals or separate with neutrals	neutralizes, softens
Add black or separate with black	strengthens and brightens colors
Add white or separate with white	softens colors
Use a variety of prints, styles, and sizes	adds texture and interest
Use lots of yellow	makes a bright quilt
Use a lot of one color next to a little of another	small area takes on color of large

Glossary

Glossary

achromatic: without color; black, white, gray

advance: to come forward

analogous: colors next to each other on the color wheel

balance: a state of stability or harmony

brilliance: the intensity or vividness of a color

chroma: another word for color, the intensity of color on a gray scale

chromatic: pertaining to color

chiaroscuro: using color and value to create the illusions of texture, luster and luminosity

color or hue: the twelve distinct colors of the color wheel and their variations. Colors are defined in EQ as combinations of red, green, and blue (RGB), hue, saturation, and value (HSV), as well as in other ways.

color wheel: a circle of twelve pure colors formed by mixing the three primary colors

complement: the color directly opposite a given color on the color wheel; each color has only one complement

contrast: using two or more things together to emphasize their differences

> **color contrast:** using two or more different colors together to emphasize their differences

> **complementary contrast:** using two complements together

> **contrast of color strength**: using two colors together in proportion to their strength

> **contrast of saturation:** using colors of different chroma or intensity together

> **contrast of value:** using two or more values of one or more colors together

> **simultaneous contrast:** placing colors together to allow them to interact

> **warm-cool contrast:** using warm and cool colors together

cool colors: violets, blues and greens; the colors of sky, sea, and grass

depth: giving a two-dimensional quilt a three-dimensional look

earthtones: the brown and beige colors of the earth

expand: when an object appears larger than it really is because of its color

foreground: the main focus of the design

grade: an EQ term describing the range of colors created when any two colors are blended. Grading two complements (total opposites on the color wheel) creates grayed tones. Grading a color with a neutral can create shades, tints, or tones.

gradation: a color scheme combining a range of closely related colors, values or tones

harmony: balance of colors

> **objective harmony:** a color plan that is pleasing according to color principles

> **subjective harmony:** a color plan that pleases you

hue: the name given to different distinct colors; another word for *color*

intensity: the saturation of a color on a gray scale; pure colors are the most intense

luminosity: the illusion that elements shine or glow

monochromatic color scheme: using only one color but any number of values

mood: the feeling a quilt conveys to its viewers

movement: the viewer's eyes move over a quilt; color affects that movement

neutral: black, white, and gray (the achromatics); containing no color

> **quilters' neutrals:** pale beiges and muslin; function as do the true neutrals

negative space: background; the area not emphasized

placement: where a color is placed on the quilt (eg.: bottom or top)

polychromatic: many colored

positive space: foreground; the quilt area emphasized

primary colors: red, yellow, and blue; the three colors from which all others are mixed

pure colors: the most intense or saturated colors (the twelve colors on the color wheel)

recede: to appear to fade into the background

saturation: the purity or intensity of a color on a gray scale; pure colors are saturated colors

secondary colors: orange, green, and violet; the second set of colors made by mixing the primary colors

shade: a darker value of a pure color, made by adding black

simultaneous contrast: the effect colors have on each other when they are placed close together

spatial effect: creating an illusion of space or depth

split complementary: a color scheme combining a color with the two analogous colors of its complement

stability: exists when there is a feeling of little movement in a quilt

strength: colors have different strengths and power

temperature: colors convey the sensation of temperature, either warmth or coolness

tertiary colors: the third set of colors on the wheel, formed by combining primary and secondary colors

tetrad: a color scheme combining four colors determined by either a square or a rectangle

tint: a lighter value of a pure color, made by adding white

transparency: the illusion that colors or objects overlap

triad: a color scheme combining three colors determined by any triangle

tone: a grayed version of a color

value: the degree of lightness or darkness of a color; a light tint or a dark shade

vibration: jumpiness, a feeling of movement

warm colors: reds, yellows, and oranges; the colors of fire and the sun

Index

Index

About the Author

Susan McKelvey is a well-known expert on color who is especially interested in making color understandable to quilters. She has written several books and articles on color, as well as on other quilting subjects, such as writing on quilts and designing quilt labels. Through her company, Wallflower Designs, she designs and distributes unique quilting books, patterns, and supplies. She teaches quilting throughout the United States, and her quilts have appeared in quilt shows, galleries, and museums.

Before discovering quiltmaking in 1977, Susan earned her B.A. in English at Cornell College and her M.A. at the University of Chicago. After earning her M.A., Susan then taught English in Illinois, Iowa, and Maryland, and with the Peace Corps in Ethiopia. She has also worked as a test development manager at Westinghouse Learning Corporation.

Susan and her husband live on Maryland's Eastern Shore near Chesapeake Bay and are active in animal rescue. They currently share their home with two rescued golden retrievers and two beautiful cats, all of whom think they were born to grace quilts!